LIFE JOURNEY SKILLS: YOUR ROADMAP AND COMPANION GUIDE FOR LIFE

DAVID POWELL

Published in Australia

This edition first published July 2003. Revised November 2022.

2003 David R J Powell

National Library of Australia

Cataloguing-in-Publication entry:

Powell, David R J.

Life Journey Skills

Published by: Motion Media International

Typesetting & Assembly: Motion Media International

ISBN Digital: 978-1-925919-53-0

ISBN Print: 978-1-925919-54-7

1. Self-actualization 2. Self-realization.

1. Title. II. Title: Life Journey Skills

ACKNOWLEDGMENTS

This book could not have been written without the help and support of some very special people:

My parents Reg and Beryl Powell who taught me by demonstration about the vital spirit qualities of enthusiasm, commitment, freedom, inquiry and exploration, vigilance, adventure, truth, honesty, strong morals and ethics, integrity, high standards and above all persistence. My father used to say — "do your best, you can't do more." This book is the best I can do. I hope it helps you do your best to optimise your life endeavours and help those around you. My mother always cared for people in her gentle, loving way. Perhaps this book can help you care more for those you live and work with.

My wife and friend, Gabriele, whose companionship I value more than I can ever express. Finding a loyal partner to share life's journey has been a very precious gift. Thank you for your unconditional love and support. I love you.

My sons James, Nicolas and Simon who have grown up to be fine men. Thanks guys for your encouragement. I am proud of you.

I would like to recognise some of my early teachers who inspired me by their example: Harold Johnson and David Cohen — our church ministers, Paddy Waller and Dai Williams at BP, Garry O'Meally at AGL, Les Nelson at Amoco, Denis Waitley, Wayne Dyer, Tom Hopkins, Brian Tracy, Jim Rohn, Zig Ziglar, Buckminster Fuller, Barbara and Terry Tebo, Robert Prinable, Robert Kiyosaki, Allen Wright, Patricia Gillard and Ulrich Kramer.

Finally, thank you to my editor, Imelda Bergin, you are terrific! There are also many unnamed people in these pages who gave of their experience and wisdom to help you. Thank you to them also.

ABOUT DAVID POWELL

David Powell is a life skills mentor, author, and executive coach. He is the founder of The Golden Thread, a media and education company that empowers people and teams to find their way. Through online courses, workshops and media, David helps you build the essential life skills you didn't learn at school so you can stay true to your life purpose.

Born in the UK, David gained a first-class honours degree in chemical engineering at Edinburgh University and worked in the resources and IT industries for 24 years, leading many teams to success. Realising that his passion lay in empowering people, he quit corporate life and became a life and business skills trainer, facilitator, and mentor. Over almost three decades, David has helped individuals and teams in hundreds of organisations, across 30 countries and five continents, improve their lives and business performance.

➡ **www.lifejourneyskills.com**

PREFACE

Is it possible for you to create a life you love? Absolutely — and this book will show you how.

You may be struggling in life — unsure of your purpose, attracting unhealthy relationships, wondering if you've made the right career choice. Your finances, relationships and business may be a long way from what you consider successful. No matter what your circumstances today though, there is a path forward. You just need to be shown the way. And that is exactly my life purpose — to show you the way.

I have shared this empowering path with people, teams, and organisations around the world for almost three decades. Now I'm sharing with you the exact same maps and models, tools and approaches that have helped many thousands create fulfilling lives, authentic relationships, and successful businesses.

Once you tap into the creative power within you — and your creativity begins the dance with Source energy — you will succeed, it's a given. I will give you the practical tools you need for your life journey. You will come to understand who you are. You'll enjoy healthy relationships that anchor and sustain you — and attract career or business success beyond anything you thought possible. You'll discover a unique way to uncover your life purpose. I'll show you how to create a life vision. You will learn how to ignite your passion, and the passion in others, so you can achieve your vision.

One of the most important things you'll learn in this book is the secret to firing up the whole person — body, mind, emotions and spirit — in you and the people around you. Let's get to it.

I wish you every success!

CORPORATE TESTIMONIALS

"In my opinion, David is one of the best facilitators in the world. Prepare to learn, have fun, work hard and be challenged."

CEO ACACIA (AFRICAN BARRICK GOLD)

"You completely held the attention and focus of 46 senior managers over two full days. Truly amazing. Many thanks."

CEO LLOYD'S INSURANCE CORPORATION

"Wow, what an insight in to how the team can operate to our full potential."

MD LJ HOOKER

"FANTASTIC, exceeded all my expectations and all of the course attendees were unanimous in this feedback. It has re-energised all of us. I can highly recommend this course to anyone."

R&D LEADER ROCHE

INDIVIDUAL TESTIMONIALS

"You are one of a very few people who have had a profound influence on my life. Thank you."

"Your teachings totally changed my life. Thank you."

"You are an amazing metaphysical engineer. You make the really complex life subjects understandable like no-one else can."

"Thank you for what has been an amazing week. You have introduced me to ideas that will stay with me forever."

CONTENTS

LIFE JOURNEY SKILLS   **9**

UNLOCK YOUR POTENTIAL   **14**

POWERING UP THE WHOLE PERSON   15
THE LIFE JOURNEY   25
KEYS TO SUCCESS   41

PURPOSE   **48**

A DEFINITENESS OF PURPOSE   49
THE POWER OF VISION   61
WORKING WITH VISION   69

PASSION   **84**

LEADERSHIP PASSION   85
MAPPING THE TERRITORY   101
ACHIEVING RAPPORT   107
KEYS TO THE SPIRIT WITHIN   131
VALUES A SOURCE OF STRENGTH   147
BUILDING PASSIONATE TEAMS   155

PLANNING   **168**

CLEAR PLANS OF ACTION   169
THE POWER OF THE MIND   195
MANAGING A TEAM   231

PERSISTENCE   **262**

THE POWER OF PERSISTENCE   263
PERSONAL PERSISTENCE KEYS   281
YOUR FUTURE   301

INTRODUCTION:
LIFE JOURNEY SKILLS

LIFE JOURNEY SKILLS

Creating the life you love requires skills, tools, and effort. My promise is that this book will give you the skills and tools. Your part is to commit and put in the effort.

The reward? You get to lead an amazing, purpose-filled life with all of the love, success, and contribution you want. Your life, your way. Once you have these life skills and tools, you become an Enabler. You can empower others around you, in your family, your community, and at work — to do the same.

Life Journey Skills focuses on empowering your whole Being — body, mind, emotions and spirit. We will dive deep into the physical and metaphysical laws that, when combined, lead you to the life you were destined to live, the dreams you have the potential to fulfil, and the person you were born to be.

▶ BODY

Our physical bodies are highly intelligent. They know how to grow, digest food, heal and self-regulate — choosing appropriately from a vast range of chemical and biological functions. We all know that taking care of the body is very important for our fitness and health and for living a long, fulfilling life.

▶ MIND

Most of us have probably had an IQ test at some stage — the test that measures the intelligence of our minds, that inner realm of thought. In this book, we'll explore how the mind works and how the thoughts you choose to think impact your success in life.

▶ EMOTIONS

Daniel Goleman's book Emotional Intelligence focused our attention on another aspect of our inner realms and how we are heavily influenced by emotional reactions.

Our emotions are affected by things — our physical health, the thoughts we think, and our strength of spirit. Emotions can range from the slow-moving, turgid depths of depression to the free-flowing peaks of exhilaration.

Because how we feel is so important, we'll explore and provide powerful tools that will help you choose your emotions.

▶ SPIRIT

The secret to creating a life you love lies in consistently empowering your whole Being — your body, mind, emotions and spirit. We're all probably highly aware of our body, our minds, and our emotions — but what about our spirit?

So, who or what is your spirit?

The word spirit is derived from the Latin verb 'spirare' — to breathe. Your spirit is the essence of who you are — the core of your being that brings the breath of life to your body.

The emphasis is on the word 'Being' — because your spirit is the watcher, the observer, and the initiator behind the constant 'doing' of your body, mind, and emotions.

The experience and skills acquired on your life journey develops the qualities and the essence of your spirit being. Your spirit being is constantly evolving.

▶ BE — DO — HAVE

Here is a very simple formula for success in life:

You have to BE the person who can and will DO whatever it takes to HAVE what you want in life.

▶ LIFE JOURNEY SKILLS

We will tap into your spirit being, the core of you, so you can make the right choices for your life. Choosing your thoughts, actions and emotions is the key to creating a life you love.

The word intelligence derives from the Latin words 'inter legere' — to choose between.

▶ ENTHUSIASM

The word enthusiasm derives from the ancient Greek words 'en theos' — the spirit within. To feel enthusiastic about your life, you need to improve the intelligence of your 'en theos' — your spirit within.

▶ POWERFUL TOOLS

It's not rocket science. You can enhance your life skills by using the tools and approaches in this book to become who you want to be. It comes down to how you manage your body, your mind, and your emotions — and connecting with your spirit being.

Throughout the book, you'll find practical tools to improve the quality of your BE state — as well as life skills that enable you to DO what is required so you can HAVE the results and success you want in life.

These powerful tools are practical, reliable, and effective. They are a synthesis of the physical and the metaphysical, a summary of what is working for people just like you all around the world.

These tools will inspire you — and those around you — to much higher and much more rewarding levels of performance.

▶ ACCELERATED LEARNING

You may have come across the techniques of accelerated learning — using colour, music, questions, and activities to increase the speed and effectiveness of the way you learn.

Although this book can't play music, we have included many illustrations because, as we all know, a picture is worth a thousand words. We have also asked many questions to stimulate your mind and activate the latent 97 percent of your mental firepower.

If you want to reach your full potential in life, and create the life you love, you must surround yourself with people who demand more of you than you do. Surround yourself with people who will stretch you and test you and force you out of your comfort zone into your growth zone.

PART ONE:

UNLOCK YOUR POTENTIAL

ONE

POWERING UP THE WHOLE PERSON

The first key to optimising your life is to focus on empowering and inspiring the whole person, Body, Mind, Emotions and Spirit — our BMES. To reach our full potential, we need to understand how to bring all of our human attributes into play.

I struggled for years to explain, in simple terms, the hidden power of the unseen realms of mind, emotions and spirit. Many years ago, during an extended period of fasting and deep meditation on this challenge, the following metaphor popped into my head — as they say, 'out of the blue'. I saw human beings as engines — powerful 16-cylinder engines. This simple metaphor has helped many people around the world in explaining our untapped potential.

▶ 16-CYLINDERS

To develop this metaphor, let 's consider that the body, mind, emotions and spirit all contribute 'fire power' to the engine — but not in equal amounts. In my experience, working with thousands of people around the world, the contribution of people's empowered emotions and enthused spirits are far greater than that of a fit body and mind. In our 16-cylinder whole person (body, mind, emotions and spirit) model, let's consider the components of the engine.

▶ THE BODY

The body contributes three cylinders of the engine. Of course, we have to look after the body. We know that we need to nourish the body with a healthy diet, sufficient hydration, and some form of exercise most days. We are beginning to understand the health benefits of good sleep. We know that we need to manage our stress levels and relax the body and mind. How well are you caring for your body?

▶ MIND

A second source of 'fire power' is the mind. The mind is a formidable, non-stop bio-computer that operates 24/7.

I am sure you've had the experience of waking up during the night to find a personal or work problem running through your mind, or a solution to a tough problem suddenly appearing. Or, you may have been out socialising on the weekend, supposedly relaxing, yet somewhere in the background, there's a problem running.

Although the bio-computer of the human mind is so powerful, it only equals another three cylinders of the 16-cylinder engine. Just like the body. Why? Because we have two other sets of qualities that deliver amazing 'fire power' when properly empowered and inspired.

▶ EMOTIONS

Our emotions represent five cylinders of potential 'fire power' in our 16-cylinder whole person engine.

Many work environments seem to disregard how people feel. Have you worked somewhere like this? Because of the sometimes appalling treatment we experience, our emotion cylinders at best clog up or, at worst, shut down.

Expressing emotions in our relationships is usually accepted — however, expressing strong feelings at work is not so accepted. We can so easily lose the latent 'fire power' of the five emotion cylinders in the workplace because of this.

▶ SPIRIT

The enthused spirit represents the remaining five cylinders of potential 'fire power' in our 16-cylinder engine metaphor. Strength of spirit is demonstrated in such qualities as integrity, honesty, ethics, enthusiasm, and commitment. These qualities define the essence of our being.

You probably know someone who clearly possesses strong spirit qualities. This is the sort of person who, if they rang you at two o'clock in the morning saying, 'I'm so sorry to wake you up, but I need help. I've just had my second puncture, it's pouring rain and nobody will come and help me' — you would, without a doubt, jump out of bed and help them.

You might have also had the misfortune of working with someone who could not spell the word 'integrity' if their life depended on it. Their approach to ethics is, at best, dubious and they believe honesty is for fools.

Body +3

Mind +3

Emotions +5

Spirit +5

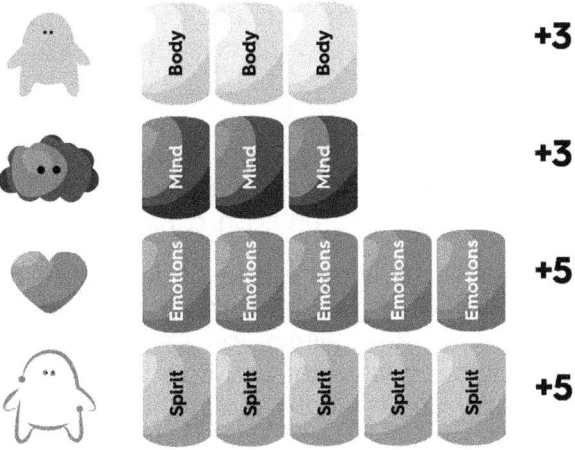

FIRING ON ALL CYLINDERS

= 16

We know when strong spirit qualities are present and when they are not.

Too often, spirit qualities are suppressed. Some people bend the truth to suit their own agenda. We may feel powerless, but we know what's going on and the cancer of cynicism develops. The precious five spirit cylinders clog up or shut down.

▶ 16-CYLINDER PERFORMANCE

In the following chapters, we'll explore a variety of tools and approaches you can use to fire up the 16-cylinders within you, your family, and your team to unleash a hidden advantage.

Sustained high levels of fulfilment and performance are elusive until you recognise and inspire the latent passion and enthusiasm of the emotions and spirit — within you and those around you. You will be amazed at what you can achieve when all 16-cylinders are fired up. It will be worthwhile and extremely rewarding.

▶ PHYSICS AND METAPHYSICS

Consider your 16-cylinders of body, mind, emotions and spirit. How many cylinders are physical? How many can you touch? The body cylinders are physical. Can you physically touch the mind, the emotions, or the spirit? No. Only three of the 16-cylinders then are physical — less than 20 per cent.

Eighty percent of our 16-cylinder engine is metaphysical — unseen and can't be touched. If you are to master motivating and enthusing yourself and other people, where should you place your focus — on physics or metaphysics?

The leverage lies in metaphysics because thirteen of the sixteen cylinders are metaphysical. So, you must understand and master the metaphysics of life if you are to create a life you love. How much of your education was dedicated to the subject of metaphysics? Exactly.

From the ancient Greeks, through to the great period of scientific discovery of Isaac Newton and his peers, on to the industrial revolution and beyond, we have refined our understanding of the laws of physics. Yet the laws of metaphysics are nowhere near as widely understood. This book aims to demonstrate how the laws of metaphysics are as real and reliable as the laws of physics. This knowledge will change your life.

Throughout the book, we'll explore a range of metaphysical laws you can rely on — not someone's opinion or theories.

▶ 16-CYLINDER TEAMS

Organisations are looking for 16-cylinder, whole-person — body, mind, emotions and spirit — performance. Would you like to live and work on 16-cylinders? It's a lot more fun! Would you like to be in a 16-cylinder relationship or be part of a 16-cylinder team? Why wouldn't you? 16-cylinder relationships are much more fulfilling. 16-cylinder teams give better service and achieve better results. Good people are hard to find. There are many people out there who are fed up with working on five (on a good day!) cylinder teams who would jump at the chance to work on a team firing on 16-cylinders. Customers like dealing with 16-cylinder staff, therefore 16-cylinder staff attracts more customers. You get the picture.

The problem is this. Most people and organisations want the 16-cylinder performance but only understand how to work with the six cylinders of body and mind. They don't have a clue how to inspire the passion of the emotions or the enthusiasm of the spirit. They are trying to achieve 16-cylinder performance from the six cylinders of body and mind — and they wonder why it's virtually impossible.

After reading this book, you will have the tools to fire up and sustain yourself — and the people around you — on all 16-cylinders. Sound exciting? Let's go.

▶ UNIVERSAL GENERALISED PRINCIPLES

Buckminster Fuller was a brilliant American scientist and philosopher with a passion for understanding the generalised principles that underpin the organising laws of the universe. He believed these generalised principles give us a direct insight into the mind of Universal Intelligence.

Because so much of the universe is invisible, his interest lay in both the universal laws of physics and metaphysics — the seen and the unseen.

If we understand how the universe is organised, we can trust and work with these generalised principles and experience success in our lives. If we work against these universal generalised principles, we are in trouble.

To empower the whole person — body, mind, emotions and spirit, the seen and the unseen — we need to explore these universal generalised principles and the laws of the physical and metaphysical universe.

These laws and generalised principles are always true and will not let you down. You can trust them and rely on them.

Understanding the laws of metaphysics will improve your understanding of you — and the people around you — and inspire them to higher performance.

We will review specific laws of physics and demonstrate how an understanding of these laws will provide insights into the less understood — but equally real — laws of metaphysics.

To optimise the three physical cylinders of the body and the thirteen metaphysical cylinders of mind, emotions and spirit, these insights are fundamental.

'I know this world is ruled by infinite intelligence ... everything that surrounds us — everything that exists – proves that there are infinite laws behind it. There can be no denying this fact. It is mathematical in its precision.'
THOMAS A. EDISON

▶ THE LAW OF PHYSICAL AND METAPHYSICAL LEVERAGE

A simple example of the correlation between a law of physics and its metaphysical equivalent is the law of leverage from Archimedes.

The diagram shows that to move a physical object, it is best to step back from the task and introduce a lever and fulcrum to assist you. So, instead of directly applying a force of 1 tonne to lift a 1 tonne weight, the lever and fulcrum allow you to stand back ten metres and apply a force of 0.1 tonnes to lift the same weight.

The task is done with ease — utilising the physical law of leverage.

Any team working on an enterprise can utilise physical and metaphysical leverage. The capabilities of the team, correctly harnessed and focused on a task, means they can do the work faster and more effectively than you can on your own.

Physical leverage

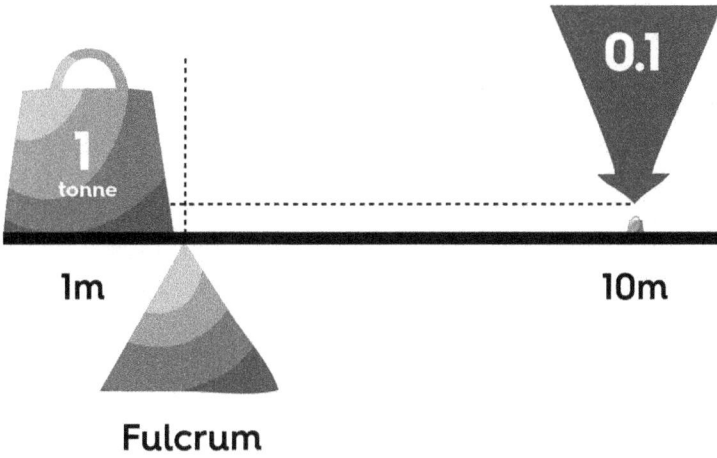

1 tonne

1m   10m

Fulcrum

=

Metaphysical leverage

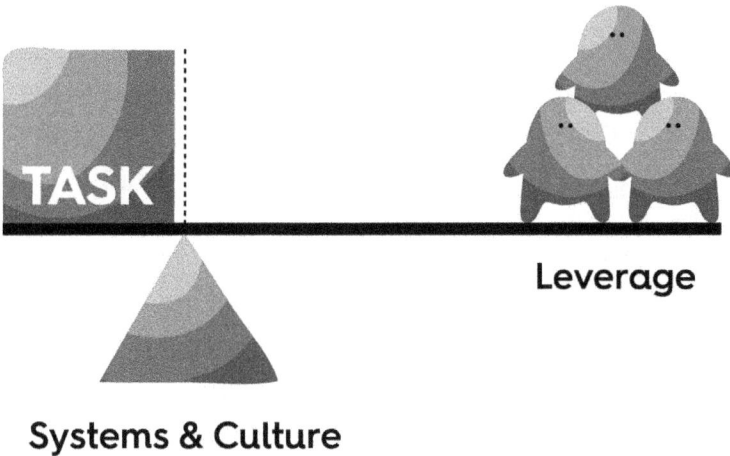

TASK

Leverage

Systems & Culture

If digging a hole takes ten days for one person, a team of ten people, provided they can work effectively together, could do the job in one day. Here we see the generalised principle of physical leverage in action. If the task was creating a complex computer program, working with the metaphysics of thought, the law of metaphysical leverage could be utilised to harness the power of more than one mind to do the job more efficiently.

A strong organisational culture and robust systems can significantly improve the leverage that a team can supply by providing a reliable fulcrum to support and enhance individual and team performance. Conversely, poor culture and sloppy systems greatly undermine performance and thus reduce the leverage of the team. We will cover this in Chapter 12 on building passionate teams.

▶ THE SHELF

A useful device to help you with new ideas — and to help you in mastery of the metaphysics of inspiring and motivating people — is the shelf. It came from an old family friend, Lieutenant Colonel Alan Hanbury-Sparrow. Alan was so old he could remember the relief of the siege of Mafeking in the Boer War. He was made a Colonel in the First World War after surviving the machine gun attacks of Passchendaele. He is passed now, but when he was in his early nineties, I asked him the secret of becoming so old and so wise, as he was both.

He said 'David, the secret is simple. It is the shelf.'

I asked, 'The shelf?'

He replied: 'Yes. In your life you will hear many ideas and concepts you are tempted to simply reject as preposterous. But the key is not to reject ideas because they seem unacceptable.'

'Everywhere you go, carry an invisible metaphysical shelf that you can put up on the wall of the room you happen to be in at the time or in your car or on the bus or wherever you are. Because if you file the outrageous ideas on your shelf, then a day, a week, a month, a year, ten or even 25 years later, you will glance up at that shelf and take down that seemingly silly or strange idea. Because of the experience you've gained on your life journey in the intervening time, suddenly the idea does not seem so silly as it did at the time.'

The key to handling ideas and concepts that seem 'way out' is to create a shelf. That's right — an imaginary shelf.

Pause for a minute and just create an invisible shelf. From now on, take it with you everywhere life's path leads you. I suggest you make it fairly robust because you may find that, as we go forward further into the 21st century and the speed of change picks up, your shelf may have to carry some fairly heavy ideas you find too much to handle right now.

▶ MODELS FOR EMPOWERMENT

These are the fundamental models to empower your whole person and enhance your life journey skills — so you can create a life you love.

- ➡ **Consider yourself a sixteen-cylinder engine. You want to access the full fire power of all sixteen-cylinders of BMES — Body, Mind, Emotions and Spirit. There are three physical cylinders and thirteen unseen, yet powerful, metaphysical cylinders.**

- ➡ **You must understand the laws of metaphysics, and the laws of physics, in relation to high performance.**

- ➡ **Anything that is too much right now, put it on your shelf.**

With these models in place, let us now look at your life to date.

TWO

THE LIFE JOURNEY

▶ YOUR LIFE JOURNEY

Before we move forward to equip you with the life journey skills you'll need to succeed in life, let's review your life journey and experience to date. This will reveal the skills you have gained as part of your personal growth.

Let me ask you a few questions. Where were you born? Where did you go to school? What was your first paid job? Maybe it was delivering newspapers in your early teens or perhaps you worked part-time after school at a supermarket? Or maybe you packed shelves in a warehouse, were a part-time gardener, drove a tractor at harvest time or worked for McDonald's?

Since that first paid job, how many organisations have you worked in?

If you've been with the same organisation for many years, how many departments have you worked in? Just pause and add them up. The number may surprise you.

> ➡ **Access our free Life course at
> www.lifejourneyskills.com**

▶ APPRENTICE / JOURNEYMAN / MASTERY

Had you been born a thousand years ago in the Middle Ages, you might have been one of the lucky ones to be born into wealth, living in a castle with the kings and queens, emperors or war lords. More likely, you would have been born into a poor family and lived in a mud hut working in the fields as a serf or peasant. In those days, your only chance of upward mobility — if you didn't want to live like your parents and grandparents — was to join a craft or a guild and learn a trade.

You might have worked in gold or silver, leather or silk, or as a stonemason or a carpenter. As an example, let's assume that you worked as a potter, or to be more precise, your parents decided you would work as a potter. When you were about eight or ten years old, they took you along to the local pottery so you could become an apprentice. That's how your career journey through life started out, as an apprentice.

Your parents introduced you to the master potter, someone of great importance, to be respected and even feared. The master potter would explain that your job as an apprentice was to do everything around the pottery that needed to be done to help the potters. You had to get up early in the morning, chop the wood, fire up the kilns, mix the glazes and prepare the clay so that when the potters arrived to start work, everything was ready for them.

During the day you would assist the potters making plates on the wheel. You would fetch the clay, tools and glazes. As they worked, they would let you practise, show you different techniques, and teach you the skills of the trade — how different clays required alternative techniques and different glazes at various heights in the kiln produced different effects.

In the afternoon, you might work with potters making vases. As they worked, they might let you practise, gradually building up your skills. The master potter was always far away, working with and advising the potters.

Each day you were up early, working and learning, finally falling asleep each evening, exhausted. The days, weeks and months passed. Potters came and went from the pottery. You learned a range of skills. Then one day the master potter approached you and explained that your apprenticeship was over and now was the time for you to become a journeyman.

You would then have left the pottery to travel the country, or even the world, working at different potteries, under different masters, using different clays, glazes and kilns as you broadened your skills on your journey towards personal mastery of your trade. Over many years, you would have developed the skills to achieve mastery — the ability to produce outstanding results consistently and elegantly.

Why introduce the metaphor of the Apprentice? Because, despite the progress of the last millennium, nothing has changed. We may live in nice houses, drive fancy cars and go on holidays to exotic destinations, but we all start out as Apprentices. We are all journeymen on a journey through life, on the road to mastery and the achievement of outstanding results — at home with our family and in our businesses.

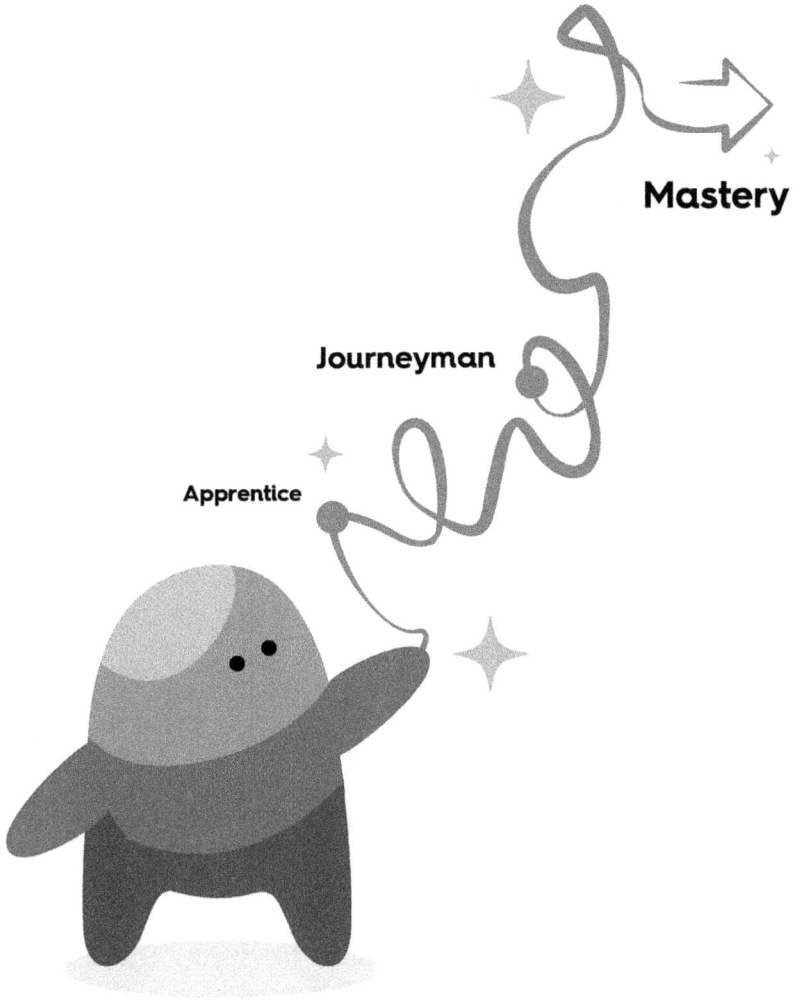

Mastery

Journeyman

Apprentice

The aim of this book is to give you the skills you need on your road to personal mastery — the ultimate destination — if you accept the challenge!

▶ REVIEWING YOUR LIFE JOURNEY

How are you progressing on your life journey so far?

If you counted the organisations, or the departments within one organisation, where you have been employed, how many 'potteries' or places have you worked in? Include any part-time jobs you had when you were at school too.

How many? Two, six, over ten?

As I mentioned in the Introduction, it is the experiences gained and the skills developed from everything you have done in your life that develop the qualities and the essence of your spirit being. Who you are, your spirit being, is constantly developing and evolving, reflecting your experiences on the journey of life.

Life Skills Inventory

To help you appreciate just how much spirit growth you have achieved, list all the skills you have gained on your life journey so far.

Take a sheet of paper, divide it up into blocks of five years for your life so far (1-5 years, 6-10 years, etc.) and list the skills you have learned in each phase of your life. You can start with the infant skills of learning to walk and talk, through to childhood skills of making friends and riding a bicycle. Then list your adult life skills such as problem solving, planning, relationships, management, etc.

I'm guessing it's an extensive — and even impressive — list!

Life Masters

On your life journey, how many masters have you had the privilege of being apprenticed to? What people would you describe as your mentors or role models?

Who has inspired you in the way they handled other people?

Who has shown you how to realise the full potential inside of you and the people around you? Has anyone been a role model for a good relationship or marriage? Who demonstrated a way to raise an inspired family? In business, was anyone you worked for outstanding at developing team spirit which led to high performance and excellent results?

Think about it and note down their names. It may be a short list.

Were there any 'anti-masters' along the way? People who you watched and thought, 'I'm never doing it that way!'

People's journey stories are fascinating. Some of us have had the privilege of meeting and working with several masters, some have worked for one or two, and others have completed their journeys so far without ever meeting a single master. What a joy it is to work with someone capable of developing high performance people and demonstrating consistently excellent results.

Many people working together are so busy that they have never taken the time to discover each other's life journeys. Powerful team building at work can be exactly that — taking the time to give everyone five minutes to tell the story of their journey through life. Try it with your team. I guarantee you'll have some real surprises, discovering where some of your people have been before they joined your organisation.

Irrespective of where your journey through life has taken you, irrespective of whether you have had the privilege of being apprenticed to masters, this book gives you mastery tools you'll need to improve your performance — and the performance of those around you.

▶ MY LIFE JOURNEY

It might help if you knew something of my life journey, both my working life and my personal experiences.

I was born in Loughton in the south of England in 1947, went to school locally and then to the City of London School. My working journey started with my first paid job in 1960. I was 13 and selling flowers in our local flower shop. Holiday jobs included stints at Du Pont and ICI, then I worked for Stone and Webster Engineering and Sainsbury's after leaving school.

In 1966, British Petroleum hired me as an apprentice. They paid for me to study Chemical Engineering at the University of Edinburgh in Scotland where I gained a first-class Honours degree. I worked for BP in Europe in various refineries and in their Head Office in London in shipping and supply.

Before I started my career apprenticeship I drove a Bedford van, with six other friends, to Greece and Turkey. In 1966, driving through Europe and across communist Yugoslavia and Romania, was an exciting adventure. When we reached Turkey, we met hippies returning from India and Nepal and I had the idea to one day drive to India and beyond.

An engineering colleague and I purchased an old Land Rover which we bought in a scrap yard in Glasgow for 50 pounds. We proudly towed it all the way back to Edinburgh and spent a couple of years rebuilding and refurbishing it.

In 1971-72, we spent a year driving overland from London to India and Nepal and then on to Australia — where I have mostly lived and worked ever since. Initially, I worked for the Australian Gaslight Company and then Amoco, Standard Oil of Indiana.

In 1984, when BP bought out Amoco in Australia, I made a major journey shift and moved into the computing industry, joining ICL, the British computer company. It was as a general manager of ICL that I first became interested in corporate education. By 1987, the mainframe computer industry was facing significant revenue issues. Downsizing and retrenchments were becoming common. I took over a group of 200 people who had suffered two rounds of retrenchments. Sales targets for my group were extraordinarily high — and morale was equally low!

Something had to be done. As the new General Manager, I introduced some motivational team building, leadership, and sales training. You can probably guess what else ICL had cut besides the head count. Yes, the training budget! So, I was forced to take off my general management hat and put on the training manager's hat. If I didn't do the training, it would not happen. The results were excellent, and we exceeded our budget targets.

ICL reorganised again with another round of retrenchments. I inherited a new group of demoralised people, this time spread out across Australia. Once more, if I did not do the training, nobody would. We again produced outstanding results, 200 per cent of budget target!

In 1990, I took on the role of General Manager at Tandem Computers, a Californian computer company. Training budgets were tight. I ran the dual role of GM and Training Manager for my team. Again, we performed exceptionally well.

By 1993, I realised my true passion lay in corporate education. So, I left Tandem and formed my own executive training and facilitation company — Corporate Leadership.

My personal journey

Driving overland to Australia from Europe through the Middle East, India, Nepal, and Thailand was a powerful experience. The spiritual focus and teachings of the Eastern religions of Hinduism and Buddhism were so different from the Protestant Congregationalism of my family in England.

My father, Reg Powell, was a Protestant Christian, a free thinker with little time for orthodox dogma. Already possessing an extensive knowledge of the Bible, he spent most of the Second World War in Palestine and the Middle East. For him, the Bible became a living geography. I remember countless Sunday lunches after church where he engaged the family in his grappling with the New Testament scriptures. What happened at the feeding of the 5000; changing water into wine; walking on water? What is the significance of a miracle? Is it supernatural power or a deep metaphor or both? If we had the faith, could we really move mountains? What does faith mean for our lives? What's the message? Questions and more questions.

This sort of thinking and discussion is not a priority for any teenager, but my father's deep questioning gave me a zest for challenging what's presented as dogma.

When I arrived in Australia in 1972, I set out on what could best be described as a personal journey of discovery and development. I studied yoga and meditation, and psychology at Macquarie University in Sydney. I read book after book on Eastern philosophy and gnostic Christianity. I attended many personal development courses and listened to hours of audio material on every aspect of self-development. In 1975, my wife and I even went to live with a yoga teacher in Sri Lanka for several months. I was continuously searching for the keys to a successful and fulfilling life.

The journeys merge

In the early days of my business, my experiments in bringing my personal development experience into the corporate training environment were considered unusual. However, they delivered powerful results and fuelled a very successful, 28-year career in corporate training.

The focus in business today is on the customer experience, customer value and customer loyalty. The key to achieving and sustaining outstanding results in any organisation lies in the potential of the staff. It is their creativity and innovation, their ability to respond to the customer in new and value enhancing ways that will drive success.

Developing and enhancing the whole person — body, mind, emotions and spirit (BMES) — is a vital skill. Because 13 of the 16 BMES cylinders are invisible, you need to become a metaphysical engineer. This book will show you how.

I don't claim for a moment to be a master, but I am an experienced journeyman. I have been happily married for a long time, I've raised a family, I've managed many business teams where we've had a lot of fun, powered up and got the job done against the odds with excellent results. I ran my own successful, global consulting business for 28 plus years.

Now it's time for me to share my knowledge and experience with you so you can create a life you love — your way!

▶ THE GAME OF LIFE

Understanding people is a vital key to success in life, so let's first look at all the people on planet earth. Our world population is 7.8 billion. The United Nations estimates that the population grows by over 80 million every year and will be over 8.5 billion by 2030.

This means that 250,000 extra people are showing up every day. Every second of every hour of every day, roughly ten people die and 13 people are born. So, every second, three new people arrive. The question is — what's the life game? What are all these people doing here?

Many people are living in sub-standard conditions and their life game is survival, worrying only about today's food. Two billion people don't even have access to electricity. But more people are playing a game called business.

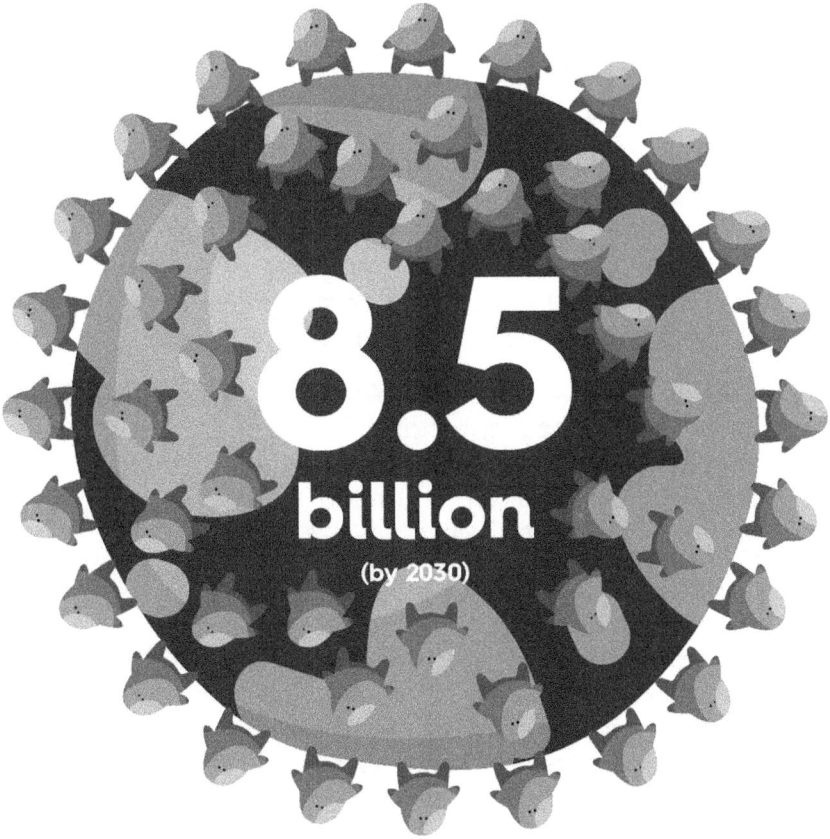

8.5 billion
(by 2030)

▶ THE GAME OF BUSINESS

The game of business can be played at many levels — from large corporations to family businesses, government, and non-profit organisations. It is a game of providing the benefits of goods and services at a competitive price to consumers and customers.

Almost everyone is involved in the game of business. In any business, money comes in and money goes out, goods and services are provided. The army is a business, local government is a business, your local kindergarten is a business, and your household is a business.

▶ PLAYING TO WIN

The game of business is tough. Many see it in terms of 'winners' and 'losers'. What is the difference between football and the game of life, or the game of business? The game of football is optional, but the game of life and the game of business are compulsory. If you have to play the games of life and business, you might as well be good at them and play to win.

The game of business requires people to be organised into teams. The general principle is that the 'A' Team is the winning team. Are you involved in the game of business offering goods and services to customers? Do you need the help of an 'A' team to improve your results and win?

Are there enough masters of life and masters of business developing high performance people and demonstrating outstanding results for us to learn from? No. They are scarce. So, we journeymen, working to fire up all 16-cylinders to optimise our life journey skills, develop good relationships, raise healthy, happy families, and build our own 'A' teams at work — are often on our own.

This book collates the best high-performance techniques, tools, and approaches so you can experience success in life, relationships and business.

▶ WORKING IN TEAMS

Some problems are convergent — the more we work on them, the more the answers seem obvious. But many challenges that await us are divergent problems — we simply don't know what to do.

What worked yesterday may well not work today or tomorrow. What worked for somebody else may not work for you. You are the journeyman. It's your journey and your experience.

Few of us work alone. Most people need the help of others to succeed. Your team can either be a formally organised group or a loose network of inter-dependent associates. The word 'Team' is an acronym. It stands for:

➤ **Together Everyone Achieves More**

▶ THE WINNING TEAM AND THE LEARNING TEAM

There are only two teams — the winning team and the learning team. If you want to become a master and consistently play on the winning team, you first have to be on the learning team. That's why the metaphor of the journeyman is so powerful. The learning team learns by making mistakes. There are no short cuts — masters have simply made more mistakes than we have.

You may have heard these statistics. A plane en-route from Sydney to Singapore is only on course about 3 per cent of the time. For 97 per cent of the flight, the plane is slightly off course with the inboard computers correcting — left aileron, right rudder, continually adjusting.

Thomas Edison, in his search for a light bulb that worked, reported over 10,000 light bulb experiments that failed before he succeeded. You have to have the courage and tenacity to make and admit your mistakes, extract what you can learn and move on. It's only when you deny your mistakes that you don't progress on your journey to life mastery.

At school, we were given a tick for being right and an 'x' for being wrong. We are penalised — if not humiliated — every time we make a mistake and conditioned to believe that mistakes are bad. Getting it right is good.

Well, getting it right is good, but making a mistake should be a — 'Whoopee, a mistake, a mis-understood. What is it I can learn from this mis-understood?' Because if you leave a 'mis-understood' unhandled, it clogs your mind. It slows you down and stops you from learning. A mistake needs to be admitted and learnt from.

T — Together
E — Everyone
A — Achieves
M — More

Look at the progression:

- ➡ **Success is a function of good judgment.**

- ➡ **Good judgment is a function of experience.**

- ➡ **Experience is a function of poor judgment and making mistakes.**

- ➡ **Mistakes come from acting, getting feedback and learning. The only real mistake is to deny the mistakes and thus their lessons.**

In my experience, most organisations are intolerant of mistakes. However, there is a brilliant story of Tom Watson Snr in the early days of IBM. A major blunder was made by a middle-ranking executive. He was hauled into Watson's office expecting to be fired on the spot. To the executive's amazement, Watson said: 'No, of course I'm not going to fire you. You have just had a very, very expensive learning experience. What we are going to do now is use that learning experience. If I fired you, I would have wasted that money.'

'Would you like me to give you a formula for ... success? It's quite simple really, double your rate of failure ... You're thinking of failure as the enemy of success. But it isn't at all ... You can be discouraged by failure – or you can learn from it. So go ahead and make mistakes. Make all you can. Because remember that's where you'll find success. On the far side of failure.'

THOMAS J. WATSON

▶ YOUR COMMITMENT TO SUCCESS

What do you want to learn from this book?

Do you simply need tools to improve your life journey skills? Are there particular angles on family or business success, enthusiasm, motivation, management, or leadership you are searching for?

List the areas that interest you. Writing these down will give you clarity – and clarity is one key to power.

▶ THE POWER OF COMMITMENT

Understand the power of commitment. Nothing happens until you commit to doing something differently in your life, your relationships, your family or in your organisation. This is best achieved by keeping a Commitments Register of your planned changes as you commit to mastering the Life Journey Skills hidden advantage tools and approaches.

As Einstein alluded to, the definition of insanity is to keep doing everything the same way and expecting things to magically improve.

To improve your ability to reach your full potential and achieve outstanding results, you must commit to change. The road to mastery is a road of continuing growth and change. It requires commitment and courage. As you read and work through this book, ideas will appeal to you that you can use on your journey towards mastery. Write them down.

▶ HARD VERSUS EASY

In life, you have to play hard or easy. Are you prepared to play hard — to tackle the ideas in this book and the actions that flow from them? I hope you are prepared for the play hard option and go for gold.

How are you going to tackle your Life Journey? Is your focus just on you, or are you also working to improve the performance of your family and your team or organisation? Are you going to commit and go for it? I hope you do — you'll have such a better time of it!

THREE

KEYS TO SUCCESS

We are all journeymen on the road to mastery. We achieve mastery by consistently enhancing our life journey skills. We achieve mastery when we know how to realise our potential, understand how to inspire the people around us, and learn how to achieve high performance and outstanding results.

Let's now consider the work of past masters. What have they done? How did they achieve enormous success?

▶ THE FOUR KEYS TO SUCCESS

There have been many people in the past who have produced outstanding results. There have been many masters of the games of life and business and many books written either by or about them.

One of the most famous books that can guide us as individuals, in our families and at work is the famous book — Think and Grow Rich by Napoleon Hill.

Over 20 million people have read and benefited from this work. The story behind the book is fascinating. In 1908, an old man, Andrew Carnegie, approached a young man named Napoleon Hill.

Andrew Carnegie made a great deal of money from steel, oil and gas. He went to the United States when he was 12 years old. He started work in a cotton mill. He never went to school. When Andrew Carnegie died in his nineties, a piece of paper, that he had written on when he was a young man, was found in his desk drawer. On that piece of paper, he had written, 'I will spend the first part of my life making more money than anybody else ever has. The second part of my life, I will give it away to who I want to'.

That was exactly what he did. Andrew Carnegie made a lot of money and then gave it away.

In 1908, Napoleon Hill was a young journalist. Carnegie said to him that he believed he had discovered the secrets of success and mastery of the games of life and business. He asked Napoleon Hill to write a book to pass on these secrets to the generations to follow.

Think & Grow Rich

A Definiteness of PURPOSE

A Burning Desire to Succeed - PASSION

Clear PLANS of Action

PERSISTENCE

Carnegie requested that, before writing the book, Napoleon Hill should talk to a few of Carnegie's friends. Twenty years and 504 in-depth interviews later, Hill eventually published what was to become a landmark text.

Among Andrew Carnegie's friends were Henry Ford, creator of the modern car, Thomas Edison, inventor of the light bulb, Alexander Graham Bell, who invented the telephone, Rockefeller, Roosevelt, Kodak's Eastman, Woolworth, Firestone, Gillette, the Wright Brothers and JP Morgan: people who helped structure the foundations of much of the social, commercial, corporate, government and financial world as we know it today.

They certainly did not succeed alone. To achieve success, all had to understand the fundamental principles of working with other people.

Why listen to the advice of people who lived more than a century ago?

We would do well to listen because these people were masters at tapping into the metaphysics of life. They explored whole person empowerment. Their four keys to success are timeless, elegant, and simple to comprehend.

1. **A Definiteness of Purpose**

2. **A Burning Desire to Succeed — Passion**

3. **Clear Plans of Action**

4. **Persistence**

▶ A DEFINITENESS OF PURPOSE

The first key to success is definiteness of purpose.

You, everyone in your family and the people you work with must be clear about what they want to achieve. What is the purpose of your endeavours? Where are you heading? What are you supposed to be doing and achieving?

A good demonstration of this comes from Henry Ford. His original 'Model T' car was built with an in-line four-cylinder engine. In 1929, after the car had been in production for over a year, he called his engineers together and explained that he now wanted a larger motor. He wanted a large motor with the eight cylinders cast in a V in one engine block for cost-efficient production. This had never been done before. Cadillac had produced a V8 in 1914 but their engines were complex and expensive, involving multiple castings.

His engineers were adamant it could not be done. Ford was equally adamant there must be a way. He held firm over many months. He had a definiteness of purpose. He knew what he wanted and why and, in the end, his engineers succeeded.

Top Tip: Having a definite purpose is the first key to any success in life. Knowing where you are heading, what you want to achieve — and why you want to achieve it — is vital.

Do you have a definiteness of purpose within you, within your family and your business or career?

We'll focus on these key questions shortly. Defining your sense of purpose is the first vital key to enhancing your life journey skills.

▶ A BURNING DESIRE TO SUCCEED — PASSION

The second key to success in achieving exceptional results is to have a burning desire to succeed — Passion.

As Yoda tells Luke Skywalker in Star Wars — 'There is no try, only do or do not'.

A good example of a burning desire to succeed and the passion to do it is the story of the conquest of Mount Everest. Everest was finally conquered in 1953 by Edmund Hillary from New Zealand and Sherpa Tenzing from Nepal. The leader of the expedition was English man, John Hunt.

The experience of those such as the Wright Brothers and Thomas Edision show us that burning desire and passion are critical. For you to achieve outstanding results, you must fire up passion in yourself — and the people around you.

▶ CLEAR PLANS OF ACTION

All successful people have a clear purpose and a strong passion. They also have the third key to success — clear plans of action. They know what they will do to get the result they desire.

Do you, your family, and the people you work with have well documented, clear plans of action on how to achieve your purpose? Are the plans good enough to sustain passion and achieve results through thick and thin? Good planning skills and tools are vital for success in life and business.

▶ PERSISTENCE

In his 20 years of interviewing Andrew Carnegie's friends, Napoleon Hill said he met many people with a definiteness of purpose, a strong passion, and clear plans of action. Yet they still failed because there is a fourth key to success. The fourth key is found in one word — Persistence.

Looking at the origin of a word can sometimes tell us more about the meaning of the word than we understand from everyday usage.

The word persistence is derived from the Latin 'per sistere' — to stand firm throughout.

All successful people say persistence is the real key.

Are you and your team able to 'per sistere' — stand firm throughout, no matter what tries to stop or block you or insidiously eat away at your morale and determination?

There is an enemy to success, and it is called resistance, from the Latin 're sistere' — to stand against you.

Have you seen the Aliens movies? The Aliens were nasty, and they grew really big, really quickly by eating humans! In the first Aliens movie, Sigourney Weaver was the hero who survived the alien menace on a distant planet.

In Aliens 2, she was persuaded to go back to the same planet with the marines. Just when they were about to radio back to Earth that the base was secure, what jumps out of the air conditioning ducts? Yes you got it — aliens!

That is how life and business can be — we encounter aliens of resistance.

How does Sigourney Weaver kill the aliens? By tickling them with a feather? No. She kills them with a big powerful flame thrower.

In later chapters on persistence, we will equip you with flame thrower strategies to help you identify and eradicate the resistance aliens as they come after you, your family, and your work team.

You've probably heard of examples of persistence. Thomas Edison and his team made 10,000 light bulbs experiments that failed before they finally succeeded and changed our night-time world forever.

Colonel Harland Sanders had long experimented with chicken recipes in the tiny restaurant of his gas station in Corbin, Kentucky. Finally in 1954, at 65, he made tentative attempts at franchising his now famous brand name — Colonel Sanders Kentucky Fried Chicken. Driving across the country, calling on restaurant owners who were potential franchisees, and often sleeping in his car, showed incredible persistence. By 1963, aged 74, he had established over 300 outlets.

The late Anita Roddick is a great example of entrepreneurship. Anita was the founder and chief executive of The Body Shop — producing and retailing beauty products that shaped what became to be known as ethical consumerism. She overcame multiple obstacles to her ultimate success with dogged persistence.

The fourth key to success is persistence. The ability to stand firm when all around us want to give up.

'Nothing in the world can take the place of persistence. Talent will not, nothing is more common than unsuccessful men with talent. Genius will not, unrewarded genius is almost a proverb. Education will not, the world is full of educated derelicts. Persistence and determination alone are omnipotent.'

CALVIN COOLIDGE

▶ THE FOUR KEYS TO SUCCESS

These are the four keys to success passed on to you — the current journeyman — by people who have demonstrated extraordinary life and business success, often in the face of tremendous adversity. They were true masters at tapping into the metaphysics of mind, emotions and spirit.

You will need to understand these four keys to success to empower yourself, inspire your family members and your colleagues so you can all achieve outstanding results.

For you and the people around you, what does it mean to have a definiteness of purpose?

To win at the game of life, you have to fire up the passions, the 16-cylinders of body, mind, emotions and spirit of you and those around you.

You have to develop clear plans of action so that every day your family and your colleagues know what they have to do.

You have to demonstrate persistence so that when the enemy, the resistance aliens, show up — you win.

As you continue reading and implementing the ideas in this book, you will see we tackle each of the keys to success comprehensively. You will become a metaphysical engineer, skilled in working with the unseen forces of mind, emotions and spirit.

Only then will you be equipped to demonstrate life journey skills mastery.

PART TWO:

PURPOSE

FOUR

A DEFINITENESS OF PURPOSE

▶ A SENSE OF DIRECTION

You can create a life you love — your way — with a sense of personal purpose that gives your life meaning and fulfilment.

The first key to success in life is a definiteness of purpose.

Do you have a sense of your life purpose?

What's important to you?

What are you trying to achieve?

Do you have a sense of purpose in your relationship, raising a family or running your home?

At work, what is the purpose of your enterprise?

A strong sense of purpose is vital to your physical and mental health, and your success in life. And it is the fastest way to enhance life journey skills. Exploring personal, family and business purpose will be our starting point.

▶ A PURPOSE OR MISSION STATEMENT

Many people experience disorientation and confusion when faced with the speed and complexity of modern life.

The word mission derives from the past participle of the Latin verb 'mitto' — having been sent.

Purpose derives from the past participle of the Latin verb 'ponere' — having been placed forth.

The question of purpose or your mission is — what have you been sent to do? Your purpose is like a marker peg placed up ahead to guide you, your family, or your work team on the journey. What is up ahead for you in each aspect of your life? What are you aiming for?

▶ LEADERSHIP AND PURPOSE

Although much of the English language is derived from Latin or Greek, the word leadership derives from a very old Anglo-Saxon verb 'laedan' — to show the way.

If you are to be a leader, you have to show 'the way'. If you are to show 'the way', then you must know 'the way'. Having a clear mission or purpose is a critical leadership trait.

This applies to leadership in any field of endeavour — with your family, in your community or your business or workplace.

Leadership means you need to know where you are heading. As they say at the start of Star Trek: 'These are the voyages of the Starship Enterprise. Its five-year mission ... to boldly go where no man has gone before'.

▶ DEVELOPING YOUR PURPOSE

Where are you, your family and your people at work boldly going? What's your purpose?

Here are some concepts that will help you with your personal, family, and organisational purpose development.

▶ COURAGE

One key to purpose development and leadership is courage — with three components:

1. **Commitment:** Nothing happens unless there is a commitment to a purpose.

2. **Action:** The leader of any group or team takes the initial action to achieve the purpose.

3. **Fear and doubt:** In my early days of management and leadership, I thought I was the only one hearing that little voice of fear, that feeling in the guts, the doubt — what happens if things go wrong? Now I realise that fear goes with the territory of leadership and purpose. If you have to lead 'where no man has gone before', then it's not whether fear and doubt will arise — the only issue is how you handle it.

The word courage derives from the French word 'la coeur' — the heart.

'We're all afraid. We just have to get to the point where we understand it doesn't mean that we can't also be brave.'
BRENE BROWN

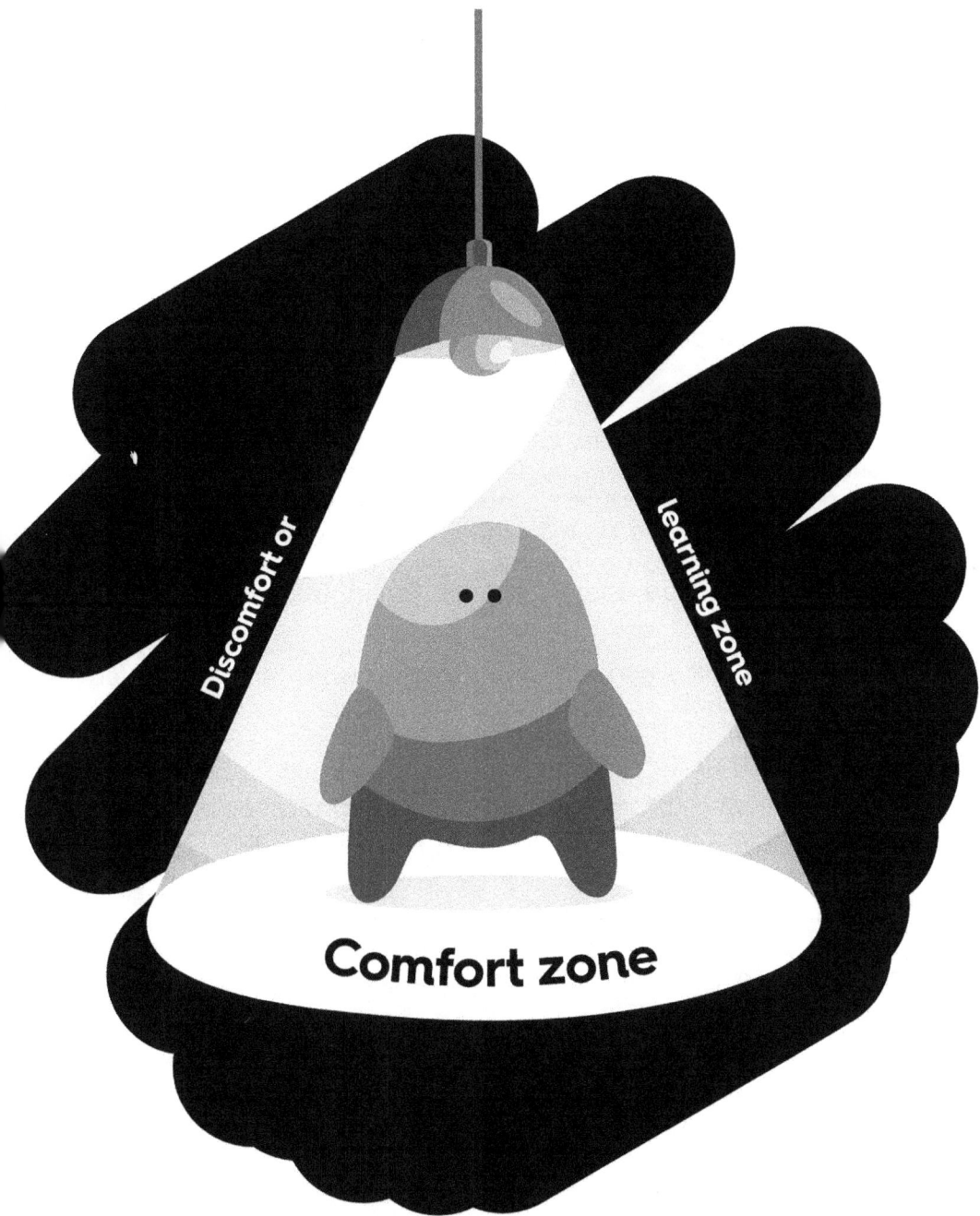

Discomfort or learning zone

Comfort zone

▶ THE COMFORT ZONE

In leading people and handling the fear and doubt that goes with the leadership challenge of defining and achieving the purpose, you may be outside your comfort zone.

You are probably familiar with the concept of the comfort zone. We all are surrounded by a space in which we feel comfortable.

In management

The word management derives from the Latin word 'manus' — the hand.

Management is defined as 'the ability to handle, control and organise with authority and skill'. You gain that skill from your life journey experience. Your comfort zone expands to encompass that database of experience.

In leadership

Outside the comfort zone, there is the discomfort or learning zone. That is where purpose development and leadership often lie: nobody knows what to do and it's up to you to lead them. The great truth of life on this planet is nobody anywhere knows what is supposed to be happening. Billions of people wake up each day and make it up as they go along. There is no grand plan!

Leaders clarify the purpose and 'show the way.' They handle fear as part of the job.

▶ RESPONSIBILITY

Whether leading a family or any other group of people, the leader is responsible for the sense of purpose of those on the journey.

Once the definiteness of purpose has been established, your responsibility as leader is then to be in service to the people — to support, empower and inspire them to do the job. Life Journey Skills will show you how.

'I'm learning that to be a CEO is to be a servant. My main job is to support our employees, and be a support to our clients and to our consumers.'
SYLVIA METAYER

▶ YOUR PURPOSE STATEMENT

In optimising your life journey mastery skills, it essential to write down, concisely, your personal purpose and the purpose of your family, team, and organisation.

Purpose gives meaning to playing the game of life and the game of business. Your purpose, or mission statement, gives you direction and meaning.

As an exercise, I suggest that you pause now and write your personal, family, work team's, and organisation's purpose statements.

- ➡ **My purpose is...**
- ➡ **The purpose of my family is...**
- ➡ **The purpose of my team is...**
- ➡ **The purpose of my business / our organisation is...**

▶ BE SPECIFIC

To ensure your purpose is focused, you must be specific.

If you listen to the way people communicate in day-to-day language, it is usually very imprecise and open to a myriad of interpretations.

What is needed for clarity and mastery are specifics.

'What's the weather like today?'

'It's 26 degrees, 54% humidity, the wind is from the North Northeast at 5 knots and the pressure is 1001 millibars and holding.'

▶ STATE YOUR PURPOSE

Take some time and re-read the purpose statements you have written down. Be specific.

Whether you call it a purpose statement, a mission statement or a vision statement, it really doesn't matter. Some people say that the purpose statement defines the destination and the mission statement defines the daily activity.

By writing your purpose statement with specific language, you achieve clarity — and clarity is one of the major keys to success.

Purpose

▶ STAKEHOLDER SUCCESS CRITERIA

For ultimate success in business and life, it is critical to review all stakeholders and their success criteria. Who has a stake in the results from your efforts? What are the success criteria of each of your stakeholders?

A purpose statement must optimise the needs of all stakeholders. Otherwise you will not garner their support — and their support is vital.

Many organisations are influenced by several stakeholders.

For example:

- ➡ **Senior management**
- ➡ **The board of directors**
- ➡ **Customers**
- ➡ **Staff**
- ➡ **Families of staff**
- ➡ **Suppliers**
- ➡ **Distributors**
- ➡ **Government**
- ➡ **Banks**
- ➡ **Taxation department**
- ➡ **Industry bodies**
- ➡ **Environmental protection agencies**

The success criteria of different stakeholders can vary significantly. Senior management may want to achieve business targets, hold operating expenses under budget, increase revenue. Environmental protection agencies want lower pollution and emission levels.

Only when you have listed all your stakeholders and reviewed their success criteria, can you then be confident that your purpose statement will satisfy them.

List all the stakeholders with a stake in the success of you, your family and your work enterprise; then for each stakeholder, write down their success criteria. When you and the people around you have achieved your purpose, how will these various stakeholders judge your success?

Time spent in reconnaissance is never time wasted. And the word reconnaissance derives from the French verb 'connaître' — to know.

Top Tip: Having completed the list of your stakeholders — and their success criteria — take the time to re-check your purpose statements to ensure they satisfy those criteria.

▶ A PURPOSEFUL BEGINNING

How effective is your purpose statement?

A written purpose statement may not be enough.

Why?

The problem lies in the way our brains process information and the way we make decisions. We are all guided by our sensory inputs:

➡ **Visual input — sight — what we see**
➡ **Kinesthetics — touch — what we feel**
➡ **Audio input — sound — what we hear**

Research shows that when we make decisions, 45 per cent of the decision is based on our visual inputs, 40 per cent is based on our gut feelings (kinesthetic) and a mere 15 per cent of our decision making is based upon what we hear.

➡ **Visual = 45%**
➡ **Kinesthetics = 40%**
➡ **Audio = 15%**

If your purpose statement is expressed only in words, it will only impress the 15% of people's audio senses, what they hear.

The other 85% of their senses, their visual and kinesthetic (feeling) processing power, will make up individual pictures and feelings of what the words mean.

Words alone therefore, are a poor medium for defining or communicating a sense of purpose.

Your purpose statement will help you clarify your thinking, but it's not enough to inspire you and the people around you.

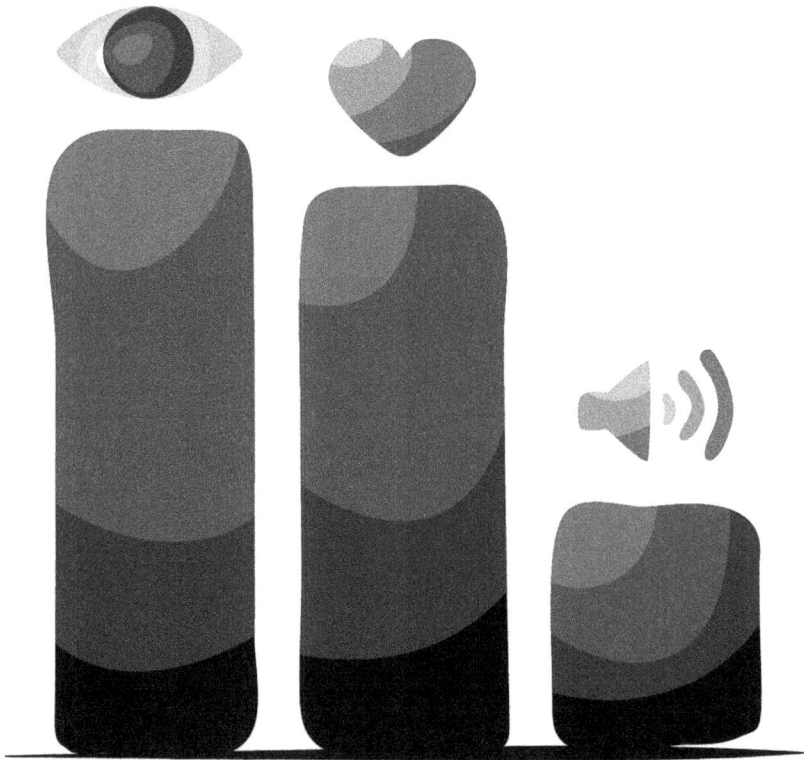

45%   40%   15%

Some people might argue that a framed purpose statement can be seen and therefore involves the 45% visual sensory channel.

However, we process written information as we read by talking to ourselves. So the problem of communicating with people in words alone, is that they hear the 15% of the words of the purpose statement and 85% of their visual and feeling senses are making up a story about what the statement means.

▶ ACTIVATING YOUR PURPOSE STATEMENT

You have to move from a purpose statement to something much more powerful. You have to give your team a picture of success — because a picture is worth a thousand words.

Writing a purpose statement does help to clarify your thinking and some senior management teams spend days, weeks or months, crafting the perfect statement word by word. However, the problem is that words just don't stick and, a week later, no-one can remember the purpose statement — not verbatim anyway. So you have to move on from a purpose statement to something infinitely more powerful — a purpose vision.

Purpose

FIVE

THE POWER OF VISION

'The only thing worse than being blind is having sight but no vision.'
HELEN KELLER

The discipline of creating a purpose statement helps you to gain clarity on what you want to achieve. However, as we've seen, words alone are not enough to fire up those vital 16-cylinders. Everyone interprets words differently — a sure-fire recipe for confusion.

All over the world, you will find organisations with mission and purpose statements on the wall in board rooms, in corridors, foyers and meeting rooms. But I could guarantee that, if you took a million dollars into your office, placed it on the table and said to the staff — 'Without referring to the company's mission or purpose statement, repeat it word for word' — your money would be perfectly safe!

▶ WHY HAVE A VISION?

People don't remember words. That is why it is critical to embrace the power of vision by illustrating what success looks like. Vision is best shown as an iconic representation of the success you are aiming for.

Vision is the first critical key to enhancing life journey skills and making better choices, to empowering and inspiring people and building high performance teams.

Every person, family and enterprise needs a vision, a picture of the success to be achieved.

▶ WHAT IS A VISION?

A vision is a pictorial or iconic representation of success. It's a picture of what success looks like in 12 months, three or five years from now.

A family with young children for example, could build a 25-year vision to see the kids launched successfully into adulthood.

► VISION AND FOCUS

Comparing a purpose statement with a vision is like comparing a light bulb and a laser beam. The average wattage of a light bulb in your lounge room ceiling is between 60 and 100 watts. If you look at a 100-watt light bulb close up, it is very bright. It hurts your eyes. But a 25-watt light bulb glows relatively dimly. However, if you look at a 25-watt laser, it will burn a hole in your eye, in fact it would probably blow a hole in the back of your head — it is the same power, but focused.

If you communicate purpose or mission using only words, you are using a light bulb, because the diversity of interpretation of each team member spreads the team energy in all directions.

A vision is like a laser beam. Everybody sees the same future — the vision creates the focus.

► DEVELOPING A VISION

No single individual has copyright on all the good ideas potentially available in defining your family or work team's vision. The whole team should create an iconic representation of success.

At work, break your team up into groups of four or five people, give them large sheets of paper and coloured pens. It doesn't matter if some haven't drawn since they were in kindergarten. Their only brief is to draw what success looks like in the future.

After an hour, ask each group to present their vision of success. You will be surprised how each group develops excellent iconic concepts to represent the envisioned future. I've seen this happen repeatedly in my 28 years as a Facilitator.

When you review the themes, it will be clear that some people have better artistic gifts than others. The team can then ask the more gifted artists to produce a composite vision incorporating the best ideas and icons. Sometimes, the artists return with a composite of the original iconic representations from the groups. Sometimes they develop a synthesised vision with new icons. It doesn't matter.

The important point is that the vision constructed by the team is more powerful and comprehensive than any one person on the team could have achieved by themselves. As everyone has been involved, ownership and enthusiasm increase.

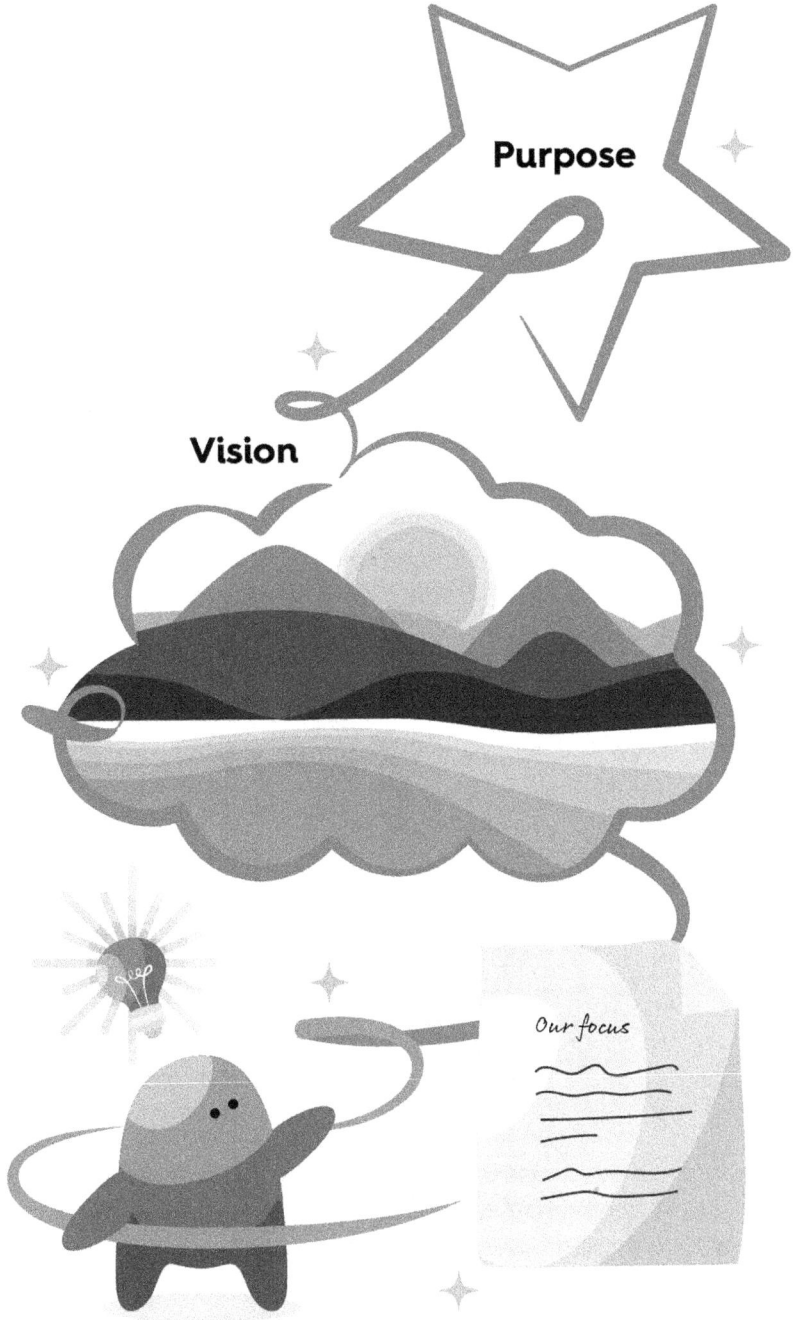

Purpose

Vision

Our focus

▶ LEADERSHIP IN VISION DEVELOPMENT

I worked with an Australian company in the finance industry. The owner's staff were extremely excited about global opportunities and their synthesised five-year vision was world-wide and much larger than the owner's view of what was possible or achievable in that time frame being discussed. His sensible counsel to his team was that their global vision was probably a ten-year horizon. A realistic three to five year horizon would be to expand into Asia first.

Over-reach

A key leadership role is to find the fine line between an enormous stretch and challenge. The leader needs to maintain team enthusiasm without setting up an over-reach that could have led to disappointment and loss of motivation.

Creating a two or three step vision works well.

In the example above, the owner and his team achieved their global vision, sooner than anticipated, by joining forces with a company with a global reach.

Under-reach

Garry and Allyn Beard are the directors and owners of a fifth generation, family owned business, AH Beard who manufacture high quality beds. They had the opposite problem. They were keen to involve their team in creating a comprehensive vision for their company. Their vision workshop was held over a weekend so manufacturing and delivery staff could attend the session. Allyn and Garry's challenge was that their leadership vision of expansion was larger than their staff dared to think. They had been involved in protracted and confidential negotiations to significantly expand their business. At that time, they were not in a position to share those discussions with their staff.

To encompass this undefined potential — and avoid under-reach — their vision contained an unspecified expansion path, backed up by excellent work from their people on what it would take to become an 'A' team — prepared for major (as yet undefined) growth opportunities in Australia and overseas.

Should Allyn and Garry have waited until the expansion negotiations were complete before involving their staff in a vision workshop? No.

As the business leaders, they needed to galvanise the entire team into a spirit of preparedness. So, when the negotiations were successfully concluded and the opportunity for expansion came, the expansion sat easily within the vision.

A lack of team consensus

Teams do not always achieve total consensus on the future vision. You may find there is significant divergence of views about the future among the people around you.

The vision exercise will draw out these divergent paths. As the leader, you will then need to work with your people to hone the potentially divergent views into a focused consensus vision.

Team reactions

During a vision exercise, the family or work team may become highly motivated and excited, because a picture is worth a thousand words. The quality of communication between people improves because you have made the effort to create a vision.

Is the vision perfect? Maybe. Maybe not. Could it change? Possibly. Is it photographic? No.

It is iconic and gives people a common language. With a verbal purpose statement, people interpret what the words mean differently. When you draw an iconic vision, and the visual and kinesthetic senses are engaged, it is much more likely that everyone will 'get it'.

▶ ICONS

Icons convey a sense of positive feeling and enthusiasm. What sort of icons show up? In business, maybe there are smiling faces for happy customers, telephones ringing, bags of gold to represent profit, shaking hands for relationships.

In a family, the icons might be a new house or car, great holidays, university degrees and world travel.

▶ TAKING UP THE CHALLENGE

Most of us share the common experience of seeing someone we recognise — on the street, or at the airport for example — but not remembering their name. Or being introduced to several people at a cocktail party and not remembering their names beyond a minute or less.

Why do we have so much trouble with names?

It is because the face accounts for the visual 45 per cent of our sensory input. When people talk and smile that involves 40 per cent of our kinesthetic senses. The name and the words only account for 15 per cent of our sensory input.

It is the same challenge with iconic visions and verbal purpose statements.

Do not underestimate the power of a vision.

It is one of the most powerful tools you can use in your life journey, especially when you involve the people around you in developing the vision. You now have a tool to fire up their unseen cylinders of emotional passion and spirit enthusiasm — at home and at work.

So I encourage you to:

➡ **develop your personal, family and work visions now**

➡ **collect pictures or create icons of the ideal new home or car or bike, holiday destinations, etc.**

➡ **involve the people around you**

➡ **use colour pens and large sheets of paper**

Next we'll review:

➡ **how reality is created from our thoughts and goals**

➡ **how to use the power of graphical vision with the deeper parts of the mind**

➡ **why individuals, families and organisations without a graphical vision are vulnerable to mediocrity and failure**

 —  =

Vision — **Action** = **Merely a dream**

 —  =

Action — **Vision** = **Passing time**

 +  =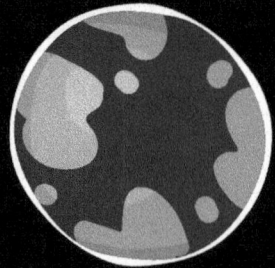

Vision + **Action** = **Can change the world!**

SIX

WORKING WITH VISION

'Dream no small dreams for they have no power to move the hearts of men.'

GOETHE

Creating a vision is the first key to creating a life you love — with great relationships, career, or business success — and a life that's full of purpose and meaning.

The next step is to learn how to use the vision to unlock your full potential.

▶ THE ABILITY TO MAKE A DIFFERENCE

Joel Barker, author of The Power of Vision, emphasises the importance of acting on our vision to bring it to reality. He reminds us we have all been gifted with the ability to make a difference and our challenge is to find our particular gifts and then work to make that difference through our vision for the future. This is equally true for individuals, families and business enterprises.

Joel Barker reminds us that:

➡ **Vision without action is merely a dream**

➡ **Action without vision is just passing the time**

➡ **Vision with action can change the world**

▶ VISION WITHOUT ACTION — MERELY A DREAM

If you have a vision of the future and do nothing about it, it remains a dream.

While at university and working with my friend rebuilding our Land Rover, we would 'occasionally' wander to the pub — as students do. We would talk to people about our vision of driving overland to Australia and even round the world. Many of them said 'what an incredible idea. One day I'm gonna do that.'

Where do you think those 'gonna do's' are today? That's right. Still back in the pub. Vision without action is merely a dream, which is why Chapter 13 on clear plans of action is so important.

▶ ACTION WITHOUT VISION — JUST PASSING THE TIME

Action without vision is just passing the time. Nothing shuts down the spirit faster than action without vision. This is true for individuals who feel purposeless.

On your life journey, have you worked in organisations where the vision was not clear? Have you worked in places where there was no sense of achieving anything other than 'ship the product' and continual quarterly pressure to make the budget numbers? It's not very inspiring, is it?

At the end of the year, even if you achieved the budget numbers, you are at best in David Bowie's words — 'heroes just for one day'. The counters go back to zero and you start again. It feels more like a grind on a treadmill than being part of an inspired team building and living a vision.

The problem is there is no 'spirit within' who will bounce out of bed every day just to achieve 'numbers' for someone else.

Numbers are useful, and can help us develop our vision, but they are not critical for inspiring people. For example, in the game of football, we keep the score by the number of goals. The only important score is at the end of the match. In the game of business, we keep the score with the revenue, profit, and balance sheet. But the numbers are merely a record of progress towards the vision. Where an organisation is just talking numbers, there's a great danger of action without vision, just passing the time. This leads to a spirit shutdown.

Many people are going through life without a vision. The lights are on but nobody's home. Their spirit seems to have checked out and they are just 'going through the motions'.

'Would you tell me please, which way I ought to go from here? That depends a good deal on where you want to get to, said the Cat. I don't much care where, said Alice. Then it doesn't matter which way you go, said the Cat.'
LEWIS CARROLL, ALICE'S ADVENTURES IN WONDERLAND

▶ VISION WITH ACTION — CAN CHANGE THE WORLD

Vision with action can change the world. Would you like to work in an enterprise where there was a real sense of making a difference? Would that be inspiring and motivating?

▶ ACTING FOR POSITIVE CHANGE

We can act on our visions in all areas of life — from the personal to the global, from the corporate to the public. The power is in the vision and the ongoing committed action that brings the vision into reality.

▶ VISION WITH NATIONS

In his book The Image of the Future, Fred Polack's question, in studying the history of nations was — 'did a nation's success follow the nation's vision of the future or was the nation's vision created because of the nation's success?'

Polack found that time and again in successful nations, a significant vision precedes significant success.

The Greeks had a vision of how they wanted their society to be. The British had a vision of a large trading empire. The USA had a vision of freedom for the individual both in business and belief. Singapore under Sir Stamford Raffles, and later Lee Kuan Yew, had a vision of a South East Asian trading centre.

What's the current vision for your nation? Do you know how your country will look in the year 2050?

Whatever the answer, the principle stands:

➡ **Significant vision precedes significant success**

▶ VISION WITH INDIVIDUALS

What is the significance of vision for individuals? Viktor Frankl wrote his book Man's Search for Meaning as a result of his experience of surviving the Auschwitz concentration camp during the Second World War.

Frankl found that although millions died, the ones who survived were not necessarily the young or the healthy, the fit or the wealthy. The people who survived the hell on earth of the Nazi concentration camps were those who had 'something significant yet to do'. They had a vision beyond the war they had to achieve. Having a personal definiteness of purpose enables us to tap into deep sources of strength. And it is vision that gave them the passion for life, and the will and persistence to survive against the odds.

SOMETHING SIGNIFICANT YET TO DO

For maximum 16-cylinder performance, and to use life journey skills in making the best life choices, you must ensure that you and each member of your family and team has:

➡ **Something significant yet to do**

How do you do that?

By co-creating a powerful vision of what can be achieved in the future.

▶ VISION INSPIRES ENTHUSIASM

The word enthusiasm is derived from the Greek words 'en theos' — the spirit within.

Would you like more enthusiasm from the people around you?

I know of no more powerful method for speaking to the 'en theos' — the spirit within — than involving your people in creating a powerful vision so that — at all times — they have 'something significant yet to do'.

Everyone has an 'en theos' — a spirit within.

Most people's spirits are battered and bruised from life's journey.

Spirits can also be cheeky. They like playing games. They also get bored.

Every leader faces a continuous critical choice. Either give the team a challenging game called 'Let 's work together to achieve the vision', or risk the spirits within getting bored and making up their own games — 'Let's cause trouble', 'Let's play politics', or worse still, 'Let's get the boss!'

If you provide an 'A' grade vision, you are setting up an 'A' grade game that will attract an 'A' grade team.

Why? Because in my experience, no one is looking for a job, everyone is looking for a game and all that comes with it — a sense of belonging, comradery and pride when the game is won. Everyone wants to be on the winning team!

Creating a vision encourages innovation, creativity and diversity of thinking because the spirit may envisage a more exciting and challenging future. Once the vision is created, people can work together to win the game and achieve the dream.

▶ VISION ACHIEVEMENT

A vision is metaphysical because it exists in the future.

Next we'll explore some of the synergies between physics and metaphysics to explain how to bring a vision into physical reality.

▶ THE LAW OF COMPRESSION AND TENSION

The generalised principle relevant to the power of vision concerns the relationship between compression and tension in the physical universe.

Wherever forces of tension exist in the physical universe, you will find forces of compression acting at right angles to the tension. Equally, wherever compression exists, you will find tension acting at right angles.

Tension and compression co-exist at right angles in the physical universe. It is a generalised principle.

If you take an inflated balloon and you apply compression to the balloon, then the generalised principle predicts that the tension will act at right angles so the walls of the balloon bulge outwards. The tension pushes them out.

If conversely, you take hold of the top of a balloon and the neck of the balloon where the knot is tied, and place the balloon under tension, or hold the two ends of a rubber cylinder and pull them apart, placing them under tension, then the forces of compression act at right angles and the balloon or cylinder becomes thinner.

If you take a piece of elastic and stretch it, does the elastic become thicker or thinner? Thinner, because the forces of tension stretching the elastic mean the forces of compression act inwardly at right angles.

The compressive forces act at right angles to the tension applied and vice versa.

Law of compression and tension

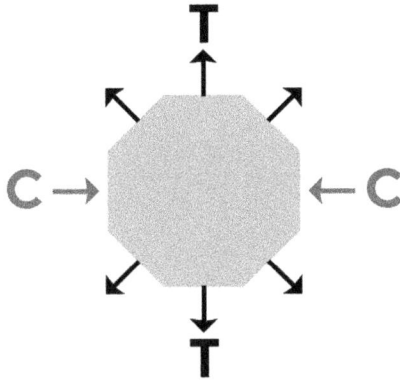

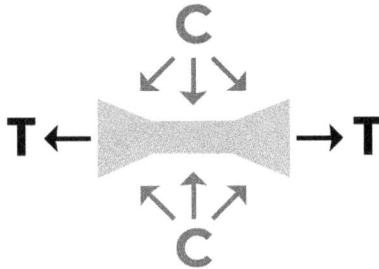

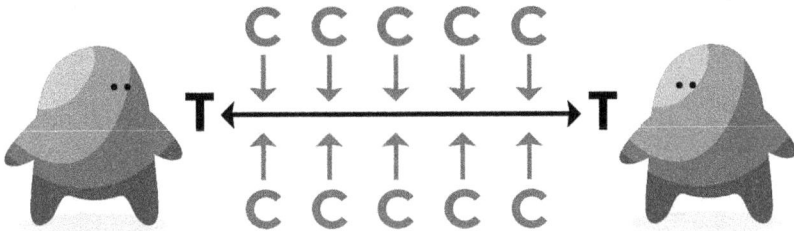

Compressive tension management style

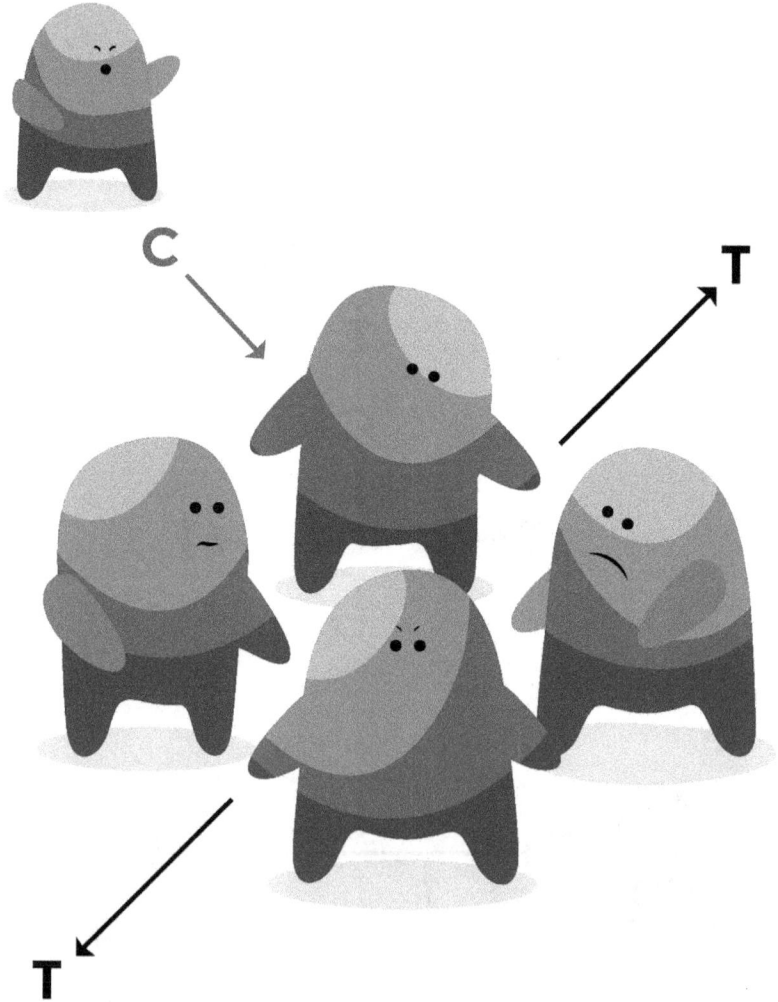

T Tension [OUT]
C Compression [IN]

Armed with an understanding of the physical generalised principle or law of compression and tension, let's now review the law of metaphysical compression and tension in the workplace.

▶ A COMPRESSIVE MANAGEMENT STYLE

A compressive style of management is illustrated by phrases such as:

'Look Michael, if you don't do that now, I can't guarantee your job by the end of the week.'

'Jennifer, tell the staff to improve performance or lay-offs are inevitable. That should get their attention.'

'George. That is the most stupid idea I have ever heard of. If your team can't do better than this we will be looking for a new team of architects.'

▶ WORKING WITH VISION

We've all met managers who use a compressive management style, pushing down on their team, suppressing their spirits. They call it assertion and discipline. If the compressive force of this style of management is applied on the team, at what angle will the tension appear? At right angles. Tension always acts at right angles.

Will the tension act inwards or outwards? As you can see from the diagram, the tension acts outwards.

Now, here is the key question. Is this force of tension, arising because of the compressive management style, pulling the team together as a cohesive whole — or pushing them apart?

It is clear from the diagram that the forces of tension are pushing the team apart. These tension forces will show up in the team as absenteeism, sickness, irritability, complaining, gossiping. Finally, people will leave.

I've observed compressive managements losing over 30 per cent of their skilled workforce every year. Imagine what that's doing to the bottom line?

▶ A POSITIVE TENSION MANAGEMENT STYLE

Conversely, you can use this generalised metaphysical principle of compression and tension to improve motivation and team work. With your team, you can co-create a powerful vision in the metaphysics of the future, a vision the team is inspired and excited to achieve.

The vision sets up a force of tension, a force that excites the team to move forward toward the future to bring the vision into reality.

The word excite is derived from the Latin 'excire' — to call out to.

As the tension of the exciting vision pulls them forward, moment by moment, the compressive forces show up inwardly at right angles. These compressive forces are thus acting inwards and binds your team together.

A vision is not only the most powerful way of speaking to the spirit within, it also is the simplest way of using a generalised principle of metaphysics, tension and compression — to bind the team together.

Enlist people to help you build the vision and, in doing so, you will enlist the help of not only positive tension, but positive compressive forces.

▶ VISION STABILITY

Another generalised principle comes into play is the need for stability. You must ensure your vision is stable because it is hard to hit a moving target.

How can you stabilise a vision?

▶ PHYSICAL STABILITY

If a physical sphere is to be rendered stable in three-dimensional space, the minimum number of restraints — to limit the sphere's degrees of freedom of movement — is 12. The sphere is held rigid at a point in space if it is secured by 12 restraints.

▶ METAPHYSICAL STABILITY

In the same way, defining the success criteria of each stakeholder, acts to stabilise your vision in metaphysical space.

This is because each stakeholder is 'pulling' to ensure their success criteria are met and their often opposing needs provide the dynamic tension and the vision stability.

Positive tension management style

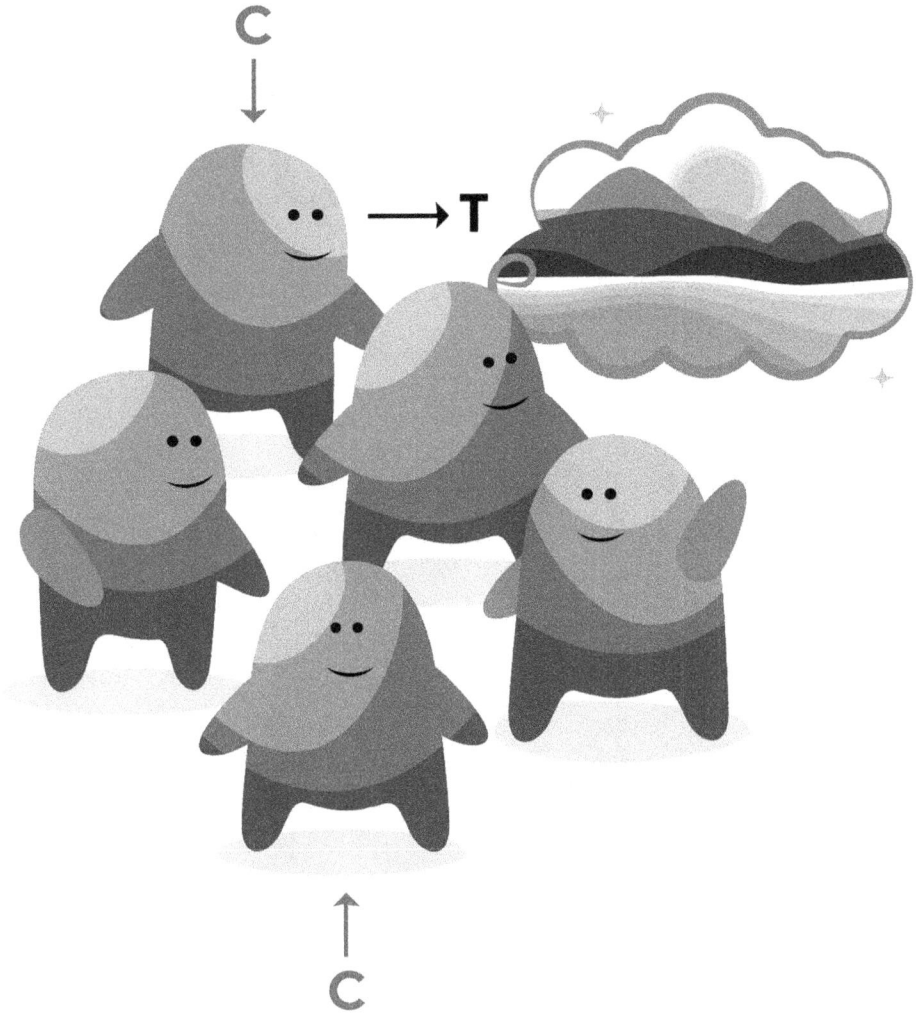

T Tension [OUT]

C Compression [IN]

Metaphysical stability

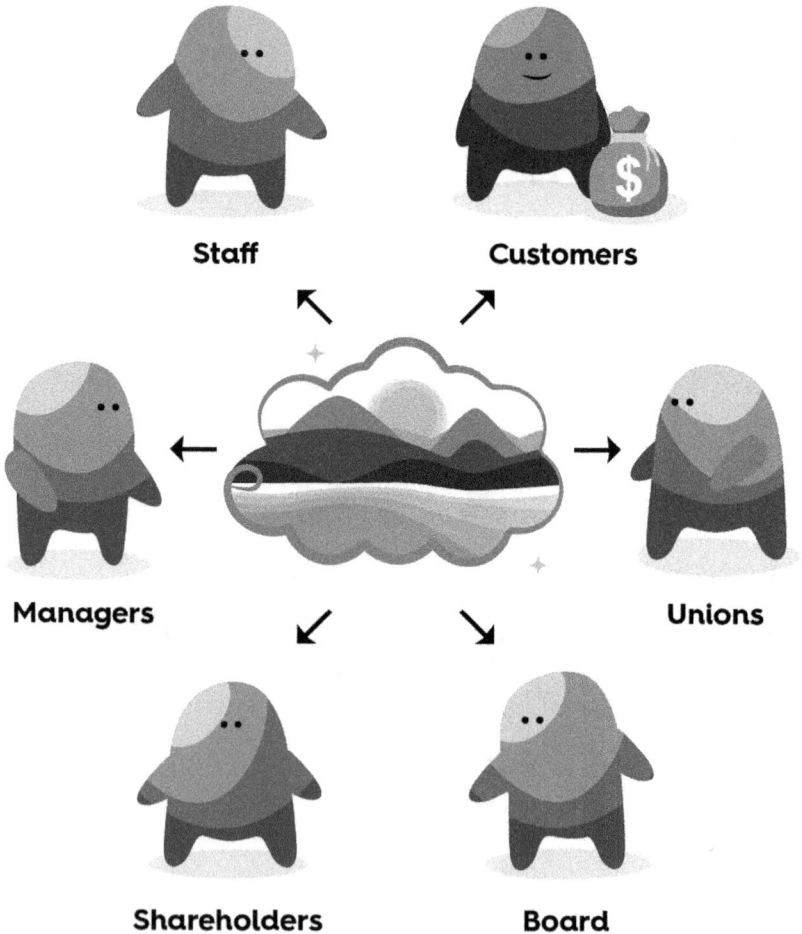

Staff

Customers

Managers

Unions

Shareholders

Board

▶ WORKING WITH VISION

Dissatisfied stakeholders will either pull harder to get their needs met, which will destabilise the vision, or they will quit and 'let go' of the vision which again destabilises it.

Most visions have nine or ten stakeholders and so can be stabilised well, ensuring the vision achieved meets all the stakeholder success criteria.

Ensuring your vision represents a balance of often conflicting stakeholder success criteria is a skill — aligning with a generalised principle of physics and metaphysics.

▶ METAPHYSICAL GRAVITY

How do you find the right people to activate your vision?

Some say that when the cause is just, the right people show up. Time and again I have seen this happen. Why? Because the metaphysical vision, once created, involves another generalised principle, the law of gravity.

In physics, Newton showed there is a force of attraction between two physical masses. A physical body such as an asteroid, when equidistant from the sun and the Earth, will be pulled towards the sun because the sun has bigger physical mass.

Similarly, once you have established your vision as a metaphysical entity, it too will attract other metaphysical entities or bodies. The right people and resources show up. Faced with choice, an 'A' grade person will gravitate to a powerful vision rather than a job or position description.

The vision has much more metaphysical mass than the job description.

We will review how to use this generalised principle of metaphysical gravity to attract 'A' grade people to your team in detail in Chapter 15 on managing people.

▶ UNCLEAR VISION

The President of a very large company once said to me, 'David. It is not possible for us to have a detailed vision of our future because we are an opportunistic commercial bank. We don't know what the opportunities are going to be tomorrow. We just know that we will be there to give better service than our competitors.'

After some discussion, we talked about the Hollywood movie Congo. In the film, there is something mysterious going on around a mist enshrouded mountain in the Congo in Africa. A fully equipped team flies in to investigate and their plane crashes. The surviving heroes salvage their equipment from the wreckage and set out to explore the misty terrain, equipped with all the latest in weaponry and laser surveillance. They need it!

I proposed that his challenge was probably similar to many opportunistic organisations. Rather than prescribing an exact desired future, the vision is the future mountain of opportunity shrouded in mist and uncertainty.

So, the key vision question is this — Is your team prepared for all eventualities? Do you have an 'A' team trained and equipped with world's best practice support systems and culture, prepared to face the future? So, when the mist clears your team can kick into action and succeed.

▶ LINKING THE PRINCIPLES

Whether you see the future of your enterprise clearly or whether you need to be opportunistic, the power of working with vision can be a huge competitive advantage.

A definiteness of purpose is still the fundamental theme. All we have done is to link that theme to the principle that a picture is worth a thousand words — and developed a vision.

The vision calls into play the generalised, metaphysical principles of compression and tension, stability and gravity.

Now we must move on to the second of the four success keys from Think and Grow Rich — passion — a burning desire to succeed. You must have the tools to motivate yourself, and the people around you, to perform on all 16-cylinders — body, mind, emotions and spirit — to achieve your vision.

Physical gravity

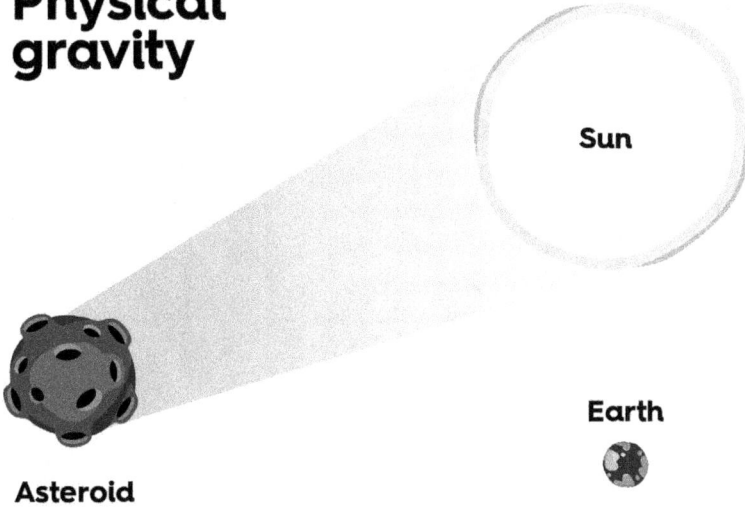

Sun

Earth

Asteroid

=

Metaphysical gravity

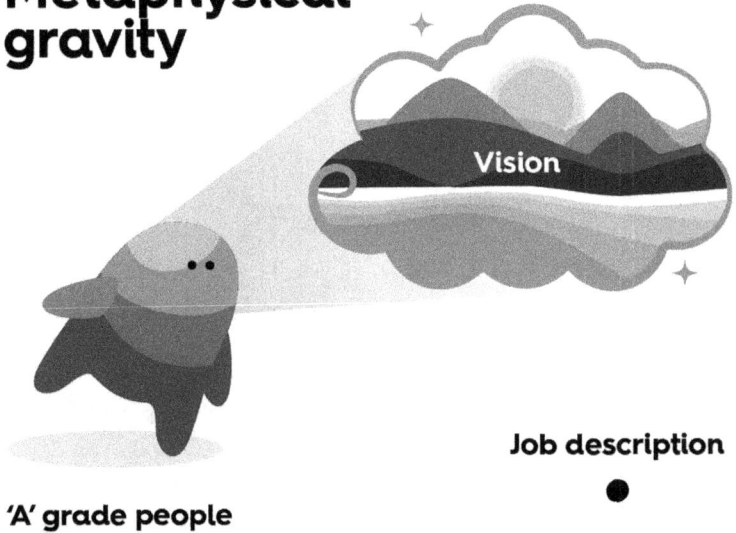

Vision

Job description

'A' grade people

PART THREE:

PASSION

SEVEN

LEADERSHIP PASSION

▶ 16-CYLINDER PERFORMANCE

What do we all have in common? Body, mind, emotions and spirit.

You have 16-cylinders of power available to you. So does every member of your family. At work, your organisation is paying for 16-cylinders in every employee. The key question is — how many cylinders are currently firing? Vision without action is merely a dream. It's people that will make it happen. So let's turbo charge you and those around you. Start your engines.

A vision resides in the metaphysics of the future, but we must achieve results in the physics of now. That is the aim of the game and — to do that — you will need inspired, motivated people to enact your clear plans of action with passion and persistence.

▶ A BURNING DESIRE TO SUCCEED

The second of the four success keys is a burning desire to succeed — passion.

Let's review your leadership role and passion. Whether or not you hold a formal position of leadership is irrelevant.

True leadership is about your passion and the image and influence you are projecting. In the following chapters, we will review how to develop rapport with the people around you and how to inspire them to 16-cylinder performance.

We will also cover the tools you need to inspire passionate teams.

Optimising high performance requires that every individual involved in your enterprises is firing on all 16-cylinders.

▶ THE UNREASONABLE CHAMPION

Being a leader is not always comfortable or easy. In my experience, if you want something to happen in life, you have to find 'an unreasonable champion' — somebody who is so passionate that they simply refuse to take no for an answer.

The unreasonable champion is prepared to persist and suffer repeated setbacks to achieve whatever they believe in and care about. In the early phases of trying to achieve your vision, that unreasonable champion may have to be you.

▶ PASSION

Look at the word passion:

- **PASS-i-ON**

As a leader, what is the quality of the 'I' you are emanating? This will have a profound influence on your leadership capabilities. Increasing your self-knowledge and self-awareness is a critical step on the journey to becoming a passionate leader.

▶ BODY LANGUAGE

You're probably aware of the concept of body language. Our bodies talk and pass on tacit messages all the time — many below our conscious awareness.

You may have observed that when people are not open to an idea, they sometimes fold their arms. Whatever the reason, they feel threatened by the idea or simply disagree with it. They don't want to 'let it in.' By folding their arms, they are blocking the flow of information.

People often fold their arms when they feel insecure.

▶ POWER CENTRES

In the East, where people are far more familiar with the concept of metaphysics, a central Hindu belief is that the physical body is sustained by seven metaphysical energy centres. These are positioned through the body and sustain our metaphysical energy and life force.

The first energy centre is at the base of the spine, the second in the region of the sex organs, the third in the solar plexus with the fourth at the heart. The fifth energy centre is in the throat, the sixth on the brow, and the seventh on the crown of the head. The Hindu term for these energy centres is chakras.

At a cocktail party full of strangers, we usually accept a drink, which we hold in front of our heart centre, so we feel less exposed and more comfortable.

If you have trouble with this concept then take this challenge. At the next cocktail party you attend, decline the glass, talk to people empty handed and see if you feel slightly less confident and more exposed.

The body language of the people you interact with will speak volumes to you if you can read it. They too will be subconsciously scanning and reading your body language. If you fold your arms while they talk to you, they will perceive (at a subconscious level) that you are not open to their ideas or that you feel vulnerable.

If you cover your power centres in front of other people, they will scan you and read that.

Interpreting body language is an art, not an exact science. People also fold their arms when they are just simply cold!

Just know your body and how and when you may be covering your power centres with your arms. These behaviours affect the quality of the 'I' you are emanating.

When you watch people, you will be amazed how people give so much away with their body language.

Being aware of body language is a vital skill.

▶ CHARISMA

The ancient Egyptians believed that each person has a spirit or Ka that survives beyond death. This Ka is the core of your being.

The Greeks postulated that at the base of the spine, you have what they called a Kharis pump.

Your fitness and the way you hold yourself — your posture — defines how much Ka you project, how much Kharis or charisma you pump out. Your posture affects the quality of the 'I' you emanate.

Rounded shoulders and a stooped posture straighten the base of the spine and shut down the Kharis pump.

Head up, shoulders back and chest out puts a curve at the base of the spine that turns on the Kharis pump.

Charisma is in the realm of the unseen but sensed — the metaphysics shining out of the physics.

Good body posture projects strong charisma. What is your body posture projecting about you?

How much charisma are you projecting to inspire other people?

▶ PHYSICAL APPEARANCE

Physical appearance is important in influencing other people.

A powerful game in our training workshops is called 'Choose the Leader'. I ask for three volunteers, task unknown!

They line up at the front of the room and I ask the workshop participants which one they would choose as their leader. They vote by standing in front of their chosen candidate. I then ask them why they chose their candidate.

The answers are always intriguing and emphasise that the 'choosers' have noted physical appearance, posture and clothes.

Grooming and personal posture are all critical leadership features.

▶ METAPHYSICAL APPEARANCE

Workshop participants always struggle to put into words how they are sub-consciously reading the metaphysics of what the leadership volunteers are projecting.

They may say the person projects confidence. When we ask them to be more specific, words do not come easily, they just have a sense or a feeling.

We have feelings about someone that are hard to put into words, but those feelings are very powerful.

▶ ZONES OF EMPOWERMENT

As 13 of the 16 BMES cylinders are metaphysical, the power of leadership passion projection is in the invisible metaphysics. There is something much more powerful than your physical stature or your body language.

**Internal Zone
of Empowerment**

**External Zone
of Empowerment**

YOUR EXTERNAL ZONE OF EMPOWERMENT

We all have something that I call the external zone of empowerment.

This zone of empowerment is invisible and can best be understood by imagining that you have a projector in your navel.

Your external zone of empowerment shines out from this projector telling the world what you are like. You can't see it or touch it, but it is there.

Other people subconsciously scan and read your external zone of empowerment because it is on — shining out in the invisible metaphysics — seven days a week, 24 hours a day.

Some temples in the East are over a thousand years old and many cathedrals in Europe are at least 600 years old. When you walk through those large studded wooden doors into an old cathedral or mosque, you can't see or touch 600 years of worship, however, you can absolutely sense a different atmosphere.

As the poet Lord Byron observed, when you go into a cathedral your soul expands as if to 'fill' the space. We scan each other at a subconscious level and 'read' the invisible metaphysics we project.

▶ YOUR INTERNAL ZONE OF EMPOWERMENT

Your external zone of empowerment is powered by your internal zone of empowerment. Your external zone is therefore a reflection of your internal zone. Your internal zone is a function of your fitness — not just your fitness of body but your inner fitness of the mind, emotions and spirit.

Fitness of your inner self enables you to develop a wide range of feelings. You can feel empathy for yourself, your family, your community and for your colleagues and your customers at work.

You can make a 'heartfelt' connection with other people. The quality of your heart shines out in your external zone of empowerment for all to see.

Inner fitness means you are playing the game of life, and the game of business, with the unseen qualities of integrity, morals, and ethics.

How you assess that is up to you. Some people have a strong spiritual set of beliefs to guide them. Others rely on their instincts.

Are you working from integrity? There are many people with no sense of integrity, ethics, or honesty. The quality of your integrity, ethics, morals, will-power, and tenacity shines out in your external zone of empowerment.

In examining the quality of your external zone of empowerment, what level of fitness do you have inside? How is your fitness of body, mind, emotions and spirit? These questions are vital for our nexus of influence.

▶ YOUR NEXUS OF INFLUENCE

Why is the concept of the nexus of influence important? Because as this diagram shows, you enter such a nexus many times a day.

Someone enters a nexus of influence with you, for example, during a formal, arranged meeting, a chance meeting in a corridor or a zoom meeting. When the meeting concludes, you will have influenced how the other person behaves during the next hour, day or week.

When do you have maximum influence on them? Before, after or in the nexus?

It is in the nexus of influence, itself.

Look at the nexus of influence.

When two people meet they bring their external zones of empowerment into the nexus.

If your zone is strong, — you are fit in body, mind, emotions and spirit and you have a strong vision, passion, plans and persistence — people are more likely to follow your lead.

Most people's minds are full of problems — relationship problems, teenage children's problems, mortgage problems, cash flow problems, car problems, health problems. Many people you encounter will probably not be thinking as clearly as you. They may not have such a strong sense of purpose — and their external zone of empowerment is weakened by their internal state.

If you are strong, people probably will follow your lead. It's much easier to be a follower than a leader.

However, what happens if your internal zone of empowerment is weak because you are physically unfit, or, mentally, you are slow and unimpressive.

What if emotionally, as John Lennon said, you are 'crippled inside', and you can't reach out with empathy to other people? What if you lack spirit fitness, integrity, honesty, ethics, and morals?

Everyone will read your external zone of empowerment and will sense the weakness of the 'I' you are emanating. Your leadership ability will be correspondingly weakened.

▶ ZONE OF EMPOWERMENT CHECK LIST

Check the strength of your internal zone of empowerment. Run a zone of empowerment audit by scoring yourself across these nine questions. Answer each question in the range 0–10. This is a classic life journey skills optimisation activity for you and those around you.

The point of power

Be honest with the questions. It is not about being Superman or Superwoman, but how you find yourself at the moment. Facing the truth of a situation is another key to power. The truth forces you into present time and your point of power is always in the present. The past is gone, history.

The future is still in the metaphysics. The point of power is now, so you need to assess the strength you are currently projecting because you cannot fool other people. At a deep level, they know it and so do you.

Question 1 — Personal Purpose

How strong is your definiteness of purpose? How clear are you about what you as an individual, a leader or team member are achieving and why?

0 is very unclear. 10 is crystal clear.

Question 2 — Personal Passion

How strong is your desire to succeed? How strong is your passion? Assess your feelings about what you are doing. How strong is your passion to succeed? Is your heart in your work?

0 is very weak. 10 is red hot and burning.

Question 3 — Personal Plans

How clear are your personal plans of action? Do you know what you will be doing over the next day, week, month, or year? Are you organised?

0 is no plans. 10 your plans are all clearly defined.

Question 4 — Personal Persistence

How strong is your personal sense of persistence? How strong is your determination to stand firm throughout? Do you have a — 'What Ever It Takes' (WEIT) attitude"?

0 is very weak. 10 is outstandingly strong, unstoppable.

Question 5 — Physical Fitness

How good is your personal physical fitness? Do you aerobically exercise three times a week for 20 minutes? Are you fit enough to run a mile? Are you eating sensibly? Are you looking after your body?

0 means you are a physical slob! 10 you are in good physical shape.

Question 6 — Mental Fitness

How sharp are you mentally? Are you on the ball and with it? Are you feeding your mind with a constant stream of education? How alert are you?

Do you have trouble thinking and concentrating? Assess your mental fitness.

0 is very dull. 10 is mentally sharp as a tack.

Question 7 — Emotional Fitness

How is your emotional fitness? Can you feel joy and sadness, elation and despair, fear and anger, compassion and love?

How good are you at emotionally reaching out and creating empathy and understanding with other people? Do you have the emotional reach to feel what they are feeling? Can you establish rapport and empathy?

How broad is your emotional bandwidth? How good are you at achieving emotional rapport that enables you to relate to people around you?

0 is very poor. 10 is outstanding.

Question 8 — Spirit Fitness

How is your fitness of spirit? Do you consciously work to maintain integrity and honesty and operate from the strength of ethics? This has nothing to do with religion or spirituality, it is about how you play the personal game of life.

0 is a very weak attitude to integrity, trust, ethics, morals, responsibility and accountability. 10 is a high level of personal integrity and strength of character.

Question 9 — Life Journey Experience

What sort of journeyman experience do you bring to the current challenge? How many organisations have you worked in? Are you experienced in the game of life and the game of business? Are you awake or asleep? Life journey victor or victim? Score your overall experience from your life journey.

0 is a very shallow, short journeyman experience. 10 is a significant journey mixture of life experiences.

Your zone of empowerment score

From these very personal, subjective nine questions, there is a possible score of 90 if you score 10 on each. Just add up your scores.

How are you doing? Is this science? No, it is art. Is your score below 40? If so, you have significant work to do. Fifty to 60? Passable. Sixty to 80 and on towards 90 is the aim for a strong zone of empowerment. Life journey skills mastery asks you to make better choices in your life and to work on increasing your scores.

This book helps you improve the external zone of empowerment, to improve the 'I 'in your passion, the 'I' that you emanating.

► YOU AS LEADER

The ultimate question for any leader is why would anyone follow you?

Management operates significantly from positional power but leadership is much more about personal power.

If people will follow you to achieve a vision, you can try mandating your managerial positional power but, the truth is, people choose to follow you — or not — because of the qualities you project.

► SUMMARY

You have by now reviewed your personal level of passion and your desire to succeed. You are projecting your zone of empowerment and the charisma of the 'I' you pass on.

Now we'll explore a range of tools to use that ensure the people around you also have the passion and desire to succeed.

To achieve your vision, you — and everyone around you — needs to be firing on all 16-cylinders.

The next step is mapping the territory that surrounds you.

'I have been lucky to meet some incredible people who do not possess what you would traditionally class as power, but through their charisma, passion, and strength of character, they are able to achieve things that richer or more powerful people could only dream of.'

HOLLY BRANSON

EIGHT

MAPPING THE TERRITORY

With a clear vision established, and your personal leadership passion optimised, the next step is to inspire the passion — the burning desire to succeed — in the people around you.

Without their passion it will be virtually impossible to achieve the vision.

▶ LEADERSHIP — NON-EXISTENCE

The first key to firing up passion in those around you is to gain an understanding of the general operating environment. You need to map out the territory, especially if you have not worked or been involved with the people before.

When you become a leader of a new team, you are in a phase known as 'non-existence'. You have no profile with the team. They may know of you vaguely — but they don't know what kind of leader you will be.

The best initial strategy is to curb the desire for immediate action and listen. Life skills mastery demands that, as the leader, you make the best choices. So first, engage in reconnaissance.

Ask a lot of questions and discover what's going on. Ask people about their vision. Some say that leadership is about asking the 'right' questions, not finding the 'right' answers. Calibrate the current level of team passion, the clear plans of action they are working with and their capacity for persistence.

If you are joining a new team as a team member, the same territory mapping principles apply. Ask about their team culture and, as you listen, map out what you are hearing. Once you have an initial map, then you can make changes to fire up their passion.

These initial mapping principles hold up every time you're involved with new people or a new team. They will also work for you within an existing team you want to take to higher levels of passion and performance.

They are just as relevant in assessing the status in your family or local community.

▶ CONTRIBUTION CONTRACTS

One of the early steps of mapping the terrain is to discover if each person in the team has a clear Contribution Contract.

Do they understand what is expected of them? Do they know the criteria by which they will be judged, and the performance standards expected of them?

Do they clearly understand the work to be done?

▶ INDIVIDUAL EMPOWERMENT

Is the team supported and empowered to achieve the results? As you scan your team members, use these three key questions to check out their individual level of empowerment:

1. **Are they able to do the job? Do they have the ability and the skills?**
2. **Do they want to do the job? Are they motivated?**
3. **Have they been given the chance to do their job with supportive systems and culture?**

▶ ABLE TO = SKILLS AND CAPABILITIES

As you explore this, work to calibrate your team member's apparent level of skills compared to what you would expect in the circumstances. You can't ask people to rise to the challenge of achieving a vision if they are not up to it.

No one can sustain passion in the face of being inadequately skilled for the task. Asking someone to play on a team when they do not have the right level of skill is unfair and de-motivating to their spirit within.

Life mastery requires that you carry out this skills audit so you can delegate tasks and train people so that you optimise passion and get the results.

▶ WANT TO = MOTIVATION

Ask questions to calibrate your team member's level of want to — their motivation.

Discover what has been motivating them to move and perform before you arrived.

Ask them to describe their vision, plans, budget, and targets. Calibrate the level of personal and joint ownership of these plans. You need to know this before attempting to move forward with them.

▶ EMOTIONS

The word motivation derives from the Latin verb 'movere' — to move.

The word emotion derives from the Latin words 'ex movere' — to move out from.

If you want your team's emotion cylinders to fire up, you need to ascertain whether they have a reason to get going. What has been motivating them to date?

Have they been subjected to management by the motivation of fear?

Fear can be a strong emotional motivator, but is not a tool to achieve long-term, 16-cylinder high performance.

The simplest way to move out from where the team is today is to give them something to move towards — a vision.

▶ ENTHUSIASM

A team needs enthusiasm.

Have they been involved in co-creating a team vision and developing a comprehensive set of action plans to achieve the vision? This defines 'a game to play' and 'something significant yet to do' for every member of the team.

▶ CONFIDENCE

The word confidence derives from the Latin 'con fidele' — with faith.

Finally, is the team full of confidence?

For people to step forward with motivation and enthusiasm and a desire to succeed, they must have faith in their leader. Has this been the case in the past?

Consider this quote from Kahlil Gibran –

'Faith is an oasis in the heart that cannot be reached by the caravan of thinking.'

KAHLIL GIBRAN

Developing faith is a heart matter. You can't command faith or prove it logically.

You can speak to people's hearts by clearly defining the definiteness of purpose and the vision, ensuring that clear plans of action are visible to all and by providing the tools for persistence.

When the resistance enemy shows up, if the people around you have the faith and passion, they can overcome all opposition and succeed.

How has this been managed before you arrived? You can't make the best choices unless you know what you have inherited.

▶ CHANCE TO = CULTURE AND SYSTEMS

As you keep talking to your team, you will get a feel for the prevailing culture and whether they feel they have the chance to perform and succeed. A resilient culture is built on trust and assertion. You need to discover which activities have been building trust and where trust has been eroded.

You also need to calibrate whether people have previously felt confident enough to speak up and assert their viewpoint. It is treason to the spirit within to ask someone to enrol in the game of 'let's achieve a vision' and then not give them the chance to win the game by denying them supportive culture and systems.

In most organisations, many crucial support systems are far from adequate and deny the chance to achieve consistent outstanding performance. Most people are remarkably resilient in working around poor systems, but it does significantly corrode enthusiasm.

You will need to decide which of the poor systems need an upgrade — to stop the treason to the spirit within and to optimise passion, enthusiasm, performance, and success.

NINE

ACHIEVING RAPPORT

'Great things in business are never done by one person; they're done by a team of people.'
STEVE JOBS

The word rapport derives from the French verb 'rapporter' — to carry across.

You need to achieve rapport with the people around you if you are to empower them, inspire their passion and secure their help in achieving the vision.

The skill of achieving and sustaining rapport with a wide range of people is a fundamental skill required for your life journey — because indeed 'no man is an island.' You cannot achieve a significant vision on your own.

Your job is to build bridges of rapport with the people around you to achieve communication and understanding and optimise cooperation and passion.

Only when the bridge of rapport is established with each person, can you consistently fire up their 16-cylinders.

▶ THREE KEYS TO RAPPORT

There are three principal keys for establishing and maintaining rapport with people.

▶ RAPPORT KEY ONE — SINCERE INTEREST

The first rapport key is simply one of sincere interest. Are you showing sincere interest in the people around you?

This is such a simple key that we need not spend much time on it. To optimise cooperation with anyone, you have to understand where they are coming from and what they want from their association with you. How else will you achieve that unless you show sincere interest?

I am sure that you have experienced incidences of insincere interest. For example, talking to someone at an office party but their eyes are wandering around the room trying to spot when the chairman of the board is free; or being in a meeting with someone who checks their phone every few minutes.

People pick up insincere interest. Either you choose to be sincerely interested in helping the people around you to fire up on 16-cylinders or you don't.

▶ RAPPORT KEY TWO — BUILDING TRUST

The second key to establishing and maintaining rapport is building trust. An interesting word, trust. What does it mean to you? Think about our whole person model of body, mind, emotions and spirit.

When you work with a new team, do they consciously know what your heart and spirit qualities are like? They may have an idea as they subconsciously scan your external zone of empowerment but they don't yet know from personal experience. The only way they can establish trust with you is by the way you behave.

Four behaviours of trust

Four behaviours build or destroy trust

1. **Reliability**

2. **Openness**

3. **Acceptance**

4. **Straight-forwardness**

Let's review and audit your trust building behaviours.

Reliability

Do you always do what you say you will do? Do you keep your commitments? Do you show up when you say you will? Can people rely on you?

Reliability is a vital quality. You are either reliable or unreliable. Which is it for you?

Openness

Are you open with people? Rapport is a bridge between you and those around you. To build rapport, you need a two-way bridge to be open to both giving and receiving feedback.

1 Reliability

2 Openness

3 Acceptance

4 Straight-forwardness

Are you open to receiving feedback? Listening is a tough skill to master. You know what they say — one mouth, two ears — that's the required ratio!

Acceptance

Do you accept people for who they are? There is a difference between accepting a person and accepting their behaviour. If you have experience with children, you will know the distinction. Little Jimmy's habit of throwing breadcrumbs around the kitchen is unacceptable behaviour. Jimmy is okay and acceptable as a person, but his behaviour is not.

It is your choice to accept each person for who they are — that is a trust building behaviour. Most people genuinely do the best they can in the circumstances in which they find themselves.

Everyone has a spirit within. Even if their flame went out years ago, you have to rekindle the spark.

Do you accept people for who they are or are you judging them?

Even if you don't say it, your judgment emanates from your invisible zone of empowerment. Be careful.

Straightforwardness

Do you say what you mean? Do you mean what you say?

Integrity and honesty are fundamental life mastery choices. People won't trust you when the going gets tough if they are not sure that you are being honest with them.

Trust Summary

Trust is built by behaving reliably, being open to giving and receiving feedback, accepting people for who they are and being straightforward.

The third rapport key is simple, powerful and easy to learn and use.

▶ RAPPORT KEY THREE — SATISFYING NEEDS

Sincere interest in the people around you, and a focus on trust building behaviours, enables you to establish a bridge of communication and rapport with each person on your team.

The challenge is that everyone is different.

This third rapport key enables you to read people and modify your approach to satisfy peoples deepest needs — at home, in your community and at work.

To explore this challenge, we will work with a model initially developed by Dr William Marston and expanded upon by Dr John Geier, to explain what motivates and affects people's behaviour.

Marston was a psychologist. While famous psychologists such as Freud and Jung were deeply interested in pathology and mental illness, Marston was more interested in the normal, healthy parameters of body and mind. In his book, 'Emotions of Normal People', he developed a two-axis, four-dimensional model that is a very powerful tool for achieving rapport — by understanding and satisfying the deep needs and fears of the people around you.

Other psychologists have developed powerful personality analysis tools, however, in my experience as an international corporate trainer and facilitator, Geier's is the best tool for rapidly reading people and achieving rapport. It is simple and practical. It works in all cultures and across all continents — because it speaks directly to the spirit within.

▶ ACHIEVING RAPPORT

Geier's analogy is that the drivers of behaviour can be viewed like an iceberg — 70 to 90 per cent of an iceberg is below the surface of the water and only 10 to 30 per cent is visible.

In the same way, we see people's physical behaviour but underneath that behaviour, sits the 70 to 90 per cent that internally drives them.

Geier explained that our behaviours are influenced by three major areas:

1. **Thoughts & feelings**
2. **Values & beliefs**
3. **Needs & fears**

Our behaviour is influenced by our thoughts and feelings. We feel hungry so we eat. We think we are late for a meeting, so we hurry.

Geier explained
that our behaviours
are influenced by
three major areas:

Behaviour

Thoughts & feelings

Values & beliefs

Needs & fears

▶ NEEDS AND FEARS

Marston's and Geier's work illustrates that we are all driven by fundamental needs and fears that critically affect our passions and behaviours.

If you are to build strong bridges of rapport with other people, fire up their passion and motivate them, it is critical that you can read and understand their deep needs and fears so that you can, respectively, meet and alleviate both.

If you have a tool that enables you to read the behaviour of everyone around you and understand the deep needs that drive them, then you can adapt your own behaviour towards them so that you build the bridge of rapport. You can consistently help them meet their needs and avoid their fears.

How are these deep needs and fears formed? You must understand this if you are to motivate people and get them firing on all 16-cylinders.

▶ WHY DO PEOPLE BEHAVE AS THEY DO?

Marston's and Geier's principal quests were to answer the question – 'Why do people behave the way they do?' As people can react so differently to the same external environment, presumably their perceptions of the environment, and what behaviour is appropriate, must be different.

Two questions

Early in life, in the first few days, weeks and months, we all have to answer two fundamental questions for ourselves.

Question One – is the world favourable or unfavourable to me?

Some people's early experiences of life seem to lead them to feel the world is a favourable place. You can always recognise these people because they become more people oriented. They like the world, and they enjoy people.

However, some people seem to find the world is more unfavourable. In life, they become more task oriented.

People > Task

So, the first behavioural axis derived from analysing people is: Is this person more people oriented or more task oriented?

Question Two — how am I going to act in the world?

The second question, irrespective of how we feel about the world, favourable or unfavourable, is — how am I going to act in the world?

Some people take the decision to become more active in their approach to life's challenges. Other people take the decision to be more cautious, a little more reserved before they act.

Thus, the second axis of behavioural analysis is: Is this person more active or more reserved?

These early perceptions and decisions reflect our deepest needs and fears. So, reading people's behaviour — whether they are more people or more task oriented, more active or more reserved — gives you a very powerful tool to understanding their deep, mostly subconscious, needs and fears.

The reason that this is so important to you as an analysis tool is that Marston and Geier found in their research that people would do anything to get their fundamental needs met. Equally, they would do anything to avoid having their fears triggered.

Relationships with people at home and at work are challenging enough without having them working covertly to get their deepest needs met. It is far better to ensure that you are achieving rapport and helping people to get their deep needs met overtly.

Using this basic four-way grid — people / task : active / more reserved — let's explore how you can use this information to improve your understanding of other people and then achieve rapport with them. This enables you to motivate them to peak passion and performance, to achieve the vision and get the results.

▶ UNDERSTANDING PEOPLE USING THE FOUR BEHAVIOURAL STYLES

When I first came across this tool many years ago, it initially surprised me to realise that people are driven by needs that are different from mine. Surely everybody is motivated to succeed and achieve results? At a deep level, people can be driven by very different basic needs. In the past, you've probably been surprised by how some people react differently to a situation.

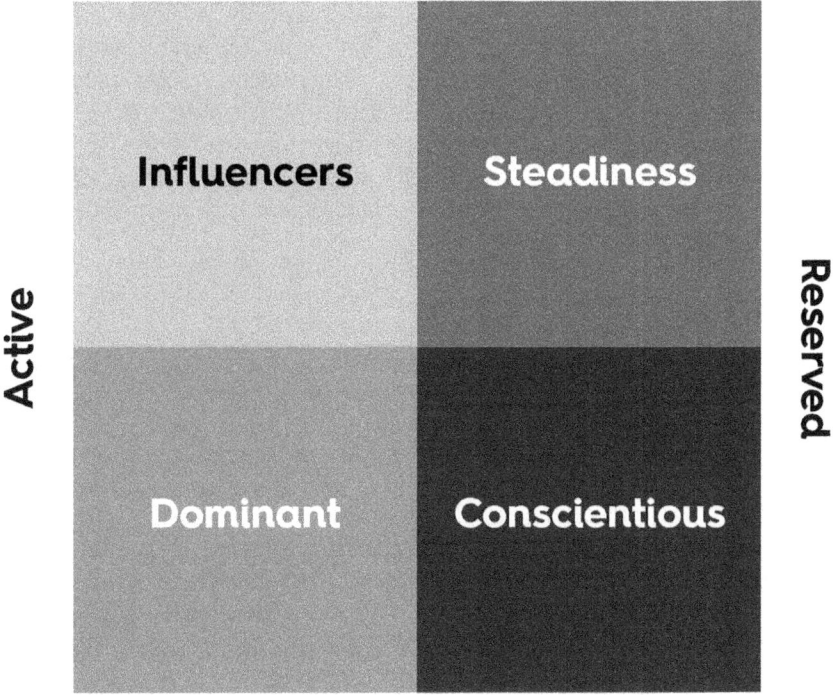

People

Active

Reserved

Task

Influencers

Steadiness

Dominant

Conscientious

Geier categorised four basic types of people with different behavioural responses to explain the differing needs and fears that drive us all, regardless of nationality or culture.

This is a universal tool for understanding people and achieving rapport and a fundamental key to unlocking individual motivation and passion. Geier nominated the four groups of people for the behaviours they displayed:

This diagram will help you to review the four very different types of people.

You need to know what motivates them, and how to achieve rapport with them, if you are to fire up their passion.

Clearly we are all mixtures of these types to varying degrees. This is a tool of empowerment, not categorisation. We can change according to circumstances but Life mastery requires you to make more sophisticated choices in dealing with the people around you. This tool helps you with these choices because it is so simple, powerful and effective on your road to mastery of inspiring passion in others.

Influencers

These people are, by nature, more warmly people oriented and active. Geier called them Influencers. They are interactive. They like people. They are always out there, talking a lot, moving around and meeting people. The more people they meet and interact with the better.

The fundamental need that drives the Influencers is social recognition. They want to be recognised, to be liked, to be involved. They want to look good. Their greatest fear is social rejection. They don't like being ignored. He called them high 'I's because of their strength in influencing others.

Using our 16-cylinder BMES (body, mind, emotions and spirit) model, it is as though each of us has two buttons, one on each shoulder.

Imagine that on one shoulder we have a needs button. In the case of an Influencer, a high 'I' active, people oriented person, their need is for social recognition. If our needs button is consistently activated as our needs are met, what do you think will happen to the 16-cylinders? Will they fire up or shut down? If the needs are consistently met, the 16-cylinders will fire up.

However, if the fears button on the other shoulder is consistently pushed, the 16-cylinders start to shut down and people become less motivated. For a high 'I' who needs social recognition, pressing the fear button would involve some form of social rejection such as criticising them in public.

Remember that people will do anything to get their needs met. Thus to achieve rapport and motivate people-oriented people, ensure they are given social recognition and praise and not subjected to public rejection or correction.

You may have been exposed to this rapport tool in the past. If not, you will be amazed at its power and effectiveness as you practice and hone this vital skill.

Dominant

There are some people who are more coolly task oriented and active by nature. They can appear very focused on the result with not a lot of time for small talk. They can appear assertive, even pushy. Geier called them Dominant people — high 'D'.

Their principle need is for control and results and they have a strong fear of loss of control because in their mind, if they lose control, what is jeopardised? The results.

A high 'D' active, task focused, dominant personality type needs control. If people will do anything to avoid triggering their fears and a high 'D' fears losing control, then guess what they do — they keep control.

Do you have people around you who are active and focused on the task, maybe less sensitive to people? Do they push hard to get the job done? Their task focus can be a great asset but sometimes ruffles a few feathers.

Clearly the way you achieve rapport with these people is different to achieving rapport with high 'I's.

Steadiness

There are some people who are also people oriented but have a more reserved approach to life. You can always recognise these people because they have a Steadiness to their character — high 'S'.

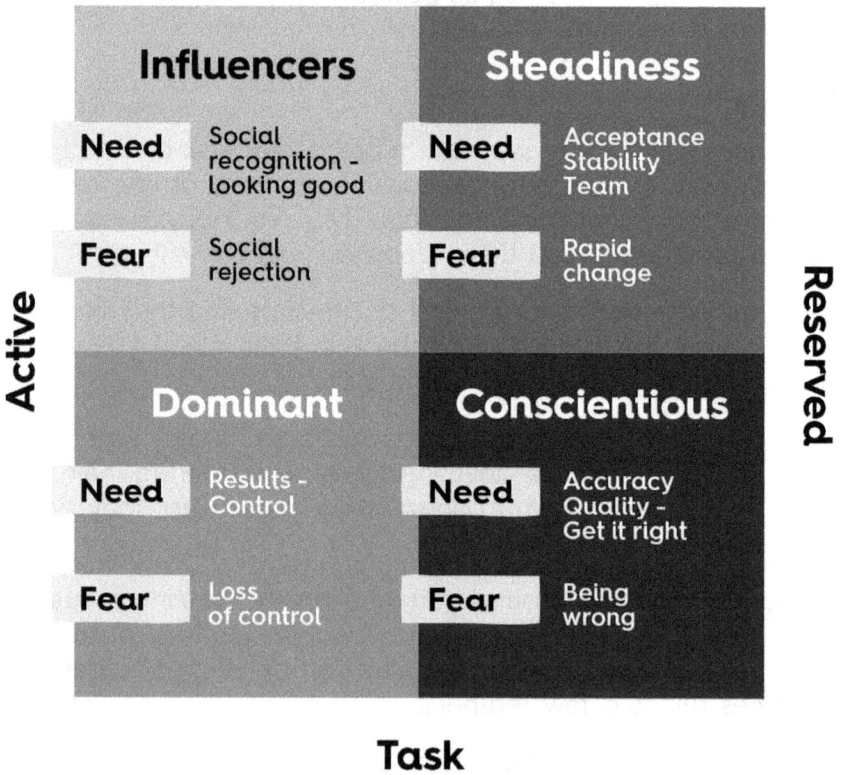

They are generally quieter by nature. They are fabulous people on a team as they are always aware of, and care for, the well-being of those around them. They have a strong need for acceptance and stability. Their great fear is loss of stability and sudden, unplanned change.

Although these people are marvellous on teams because of their inherent team building natures and the fact that they care about team members, they are really challenged by change.

What is happening all around us? Change. And the pace of change seems to be speeding up.

So, for 'S' people who are more people oriented and reserved by nature, their deepest need is stability. Their greatest fear is sudden or unplanned change. Which of their buttons is being pushed more and more? Their 'fear' button.

'S' people are very valuable as team members. You must look after them, carefully plan the necessary changes — step by step — to help them maintain 16-cylinder empowerment.

Conscientious / Cautious

There are some people who are more task oriented and yet tend to be more reserved by nature. They work long hours and are very detail oriented and conscientious. Geier called these people Cautious or Conscientious — high 'C'.

These people have a deep need for accuracy, quality, detail, and getting it right. Their great fear is criticism because criticism makes them wrong and they have a strong need to be right.

To meet their needs, high 'C' people will work back long hours to complete the work. They are detail aware. They will do almost anything to be right. They are very conscientious in their approach to life and work, setting high standards for themselves and the rest of a team.

A mixed team?

Successful teams need a mix of these different types of people.

➡ **The high 'C' Conscientious people are the guardians of detail and quality.**

- **The active, task focused Dominant high 'D' personalities are out there doing almost anything for the result — whatever it takes to succeed.**
- **The optimists, the high 'I' Influencers are active and enthusiastic. Sometimes their attention to detail is not always their strong suit. That's why you need the high 'C's.**
- **The more reserved high 'S' Steadiness people are the team guardians. They really appreciate being on a good team, they work hard to preserve and enhance teamwork even when the pressure is on.**

DISC as an analysis tool

This DISC tool gives you the clues to other people's needs. You can start to see the power of the tool in meeting needs and thus optimising passion. The diagram summarises the needs and fears of the four types of people we have looked at.

DISC graphic equalisers

It is essential to emphasise that we all have elements of the four DISC personalities, but we are dominant in one. This tool is not intended to narrowly categorise anyone. Imagine that people having four DISC graphic equalisers — they can change their DISC emphasis but have a preferred setting.

Most people have a tendency to be either more people or more task oriented in the way they approach a challenge. Some people are more active and some more reserved by nature.

To achieve your vision, you need to understand how to relate to others, and achieve rapport by adjusting your DISC graphic equalisers to match those of the person you are dealing with.

Your own DISC setting is not the important thing here, it is rather being flexible, achieving rapport and motivating and firing up passion in others.

People analysis

List each of the key people around you at home, in your community and at work. Ask yourself — is their orientation by nature more warmly people oriented or more coolly task oriented? Are they more active by nature or more reserved? How have they set their four DISC graphic equalisers?

D Dominant | **I** Influencer | **S** Steadiness | **C** Conscientious

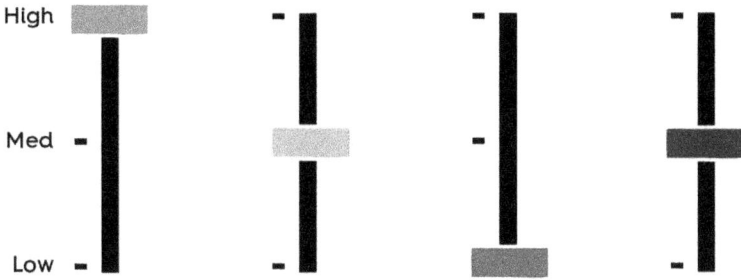

High

Med

Low

Then think about their needs and fears, as we have discussed, and see if you can discern those needs and fears through their behaviour.

If you are in a relationship, think about your partner and consider whether the model holds true for them too. Are they more people or task oriented by nature, more active or more reserved? Can you see how they get their needs met in your relationship? If you help them get their needs met, more often than not, your relationship will thrive. What about your kids?

▶ VARIABLE RAPPORT STYLES

To achieve a vision and get results, you need everyone around you consistently fired up on 16-cylinders. It will help enormously if you can establish and maintain rapport with each of them in good times and bad. This is equally true at home or with close friends and relatives.

Now we will explore how you can you modify your rapport approach to ensure you consistently meet each person's needs especially when under pressure, firing up their 16-cylinders and passion. We will also cover what behaviours are appropriate to avoid triggering their fears and shutting down their cylinders.

Building rapport with active 'D's

When dealing with active high 'D' Dominant people, speed up and keep it moving. The task oriented 'D's will want to cut straight to the chase, with no time for chit-chat or small talk.

Let's take an example. John is a young man on your team. He is very enthusiastic, keen, even pushy and always opinionated. Some people find him cold and abrasive. You like him because he can be relied on to do the job. Our model would indicate that young John is active and task-oriented. He has a high 'D' Dominant graphic equaliser. This helps you motivate his passion in two ways — first, it gives you clues to the speed of your approach to him in building rapport. Secondly, it influences the way you phrase the needs of the challenge to play to his needs and to avoid his fears.

With someone who is task focused and active by nature, your rapport style must be active. Avoid the chit-chat and move straight to the point.

'John, this task will need to be done over the next few months. Like you, I am only concerned with one thing. Getting it done. I will leave this in your hands to manage as you see fit.

Now what have you done? You have just passed control to John and pressed his needs button. You have emphasised the need for results. You have steered away from any sense he might have been losing control. You have avoided his fears. Give John the control he's looking for and he will be on 16-cylinders.

'D' under pressure

High 'D', active task people like John will become more dominant, aggressive and domineering if a stressful situation threatens their control needs fulfilment. Under extreme pressure they can become dictatorial — 'Just do it. It's my way or the highway. Got it?'

To ensure that you keep them motivated under pressure with their passion fired up, leave a sense of control with them. Make sure that they have a clear path forward with a set of action plans to achieve results.

Building rapport with active 'I's

Mary is also an active person but much more outgoing, friendly and people oriented. She is always organising team lunches and after work drinks. She is friendly and optimistic. Mary has a high 'I' Influencer graphic equaliser.

To establish rapport, Mary will want some time for a preliminary chat. If you use the same task-oriented approach as you have just done with John, she will find you cold and unfriendly. High 'I's need to talk. Try and shut them up or push the task too hard and the rapport bridge weakens. People with an Influencer high 'I' in their nature like some preamble.

'How was your weekend Mary?'

'Oh, it was wonderful, let me tell you about it.'

High 'D's couldn't give a damn about the weekend. That's past. They went sky diving or bungee jumping and that doesn't affect today's result. So why waste time talking about it?

High 'I's, however, like social interaction and, talking to Mary, your initial rapport approach must provide time for talking about how her weekend was and how she is feeling. Then in talking about the vision and the work plans, your approach could be:

'Mary, if you and your group can do the work in this area the team will love you'.

Appealing to her need for social recognition by giving plenty of praise and recognition — and a chance to shine — is the way to ensure Mary is highly motivated and in action, with her passion cylinders fired up.

If you have to, always correct high 'I's in private to avoid perceived social rejection.

'I' under pressure

Under pressure and stress, the high 'I' Influencer like Mary becomes more excited and talkative as they fear social rejection and loss of face.

If the tension really mounts, they may throw a tantrum to receive attention and have their recognition needs met. So, under pressure, reach out to give your high 'I' Influencers the recognition they need.

Don't ignore them and don't bring in negativity. Keep it positive and optimistic. You need the high 'I's on 16-cylinders — especially in the tough times.

▶ RAPPORT WITH MORE RESERVED PEOPLE

People who are more reserved have much higher acuity. They are far more observant and perceptive than the more active 'D' and 'I' personality types. However, because they are reserved by nature, they won't necessarily feel comfortable to speak up.

They are also more sensitive. This can cause problems when we consider the external zone of empowerment of the high 'D's and 'I's.

The external zone of empowerment of the active high 'D's and 'I's hits them like a metaphysical shock wave. I'm sure you've seen the large bow wave in front of a power boat. These people don't mean to project it so strongly, it is just their nature, their natural active energy. They don't notice it because by nature they are active. When cautioned they'll say — 'I had no idea I had that effect on people'.

To understand the likely reaction of a more reserved and sensitive high 'S' or high 'C' person to the shock wave preceding the high 'D's and 'I's, we can use a metaphor from the science fiction series Star Trek.

In Star Trek, who are the baddies? The Klingons. The Klingons have spaceships that can be made invisible to the USS Enterprise scanners of Captain James Kirk and his Star Trek team. However, the Klingon spaceship can't fire its weapons until the invisible device is de-activated. So, it uncloaks itself just prior to attack and thus appears on the Enterprise scanners before firing. When that happens, the USS Enterprise puts up shields to protect itself from attack.

It is the same with these more reserved and sensitive people. As the high 'D's and 'I's power around, with external zones of empowerment shock waves emanating from them, the high acuity 'S's and 'C's see them coming and say to themselves — 'Oh no, here come the Klingons — and up go the shields!

It's no surprise then that the 'D's and 'I's wonder why they have trouble communicating with more reserved people, if they notice at all! You can't build rapport or communicate through a shield.

Rapport with more reserved people requires calm.

Building rapport with more reserved 'S' types

To build rapport with a more reserved, people oriented person with a high 'S' graphic equaliser, slow down. Because they are people oriented, they also need some preliminary rapport building talk — 'Hi. How is it going? How is the team? How is the family?'

Nothing too exuberant. Nothing too long. You just need some basic, friendly introduction.

A good strategy for the more reserved 'S' personality types would be to frame up your discussion about the vision, the plan and the other team members in terms of his needs –

'George, I need your help in involving the whole team. It is critical that during this project we maintain an air of stability and teamwork.'

George will be very concerned about sudden or unplanned change. What would look like a crack in the floorboards to a high 'D' like a John or a high 'I' like Mary would look like jumping the Grand Canyon to George. He will tell you that what you are proposing is absolutely impossible. It just involves too much change. So for George, crossing the Grand Canyon requires stepping stones:

'George. I appreciate your concerns, and I've thought through a 14 step plan of action. What I suggest is we go over the 14 steps and when you are comfortable, then I would like you and your team to initiate the plan.'

You show the high 'S' person how to deal with the change necessary to bring your vision to life.

'S' under pressure

Under pressure, people with a high 'S' Steadiness graphic equaliser like George tend to withdraw. They are looking for stability — and pressure brings instability and change.

If you push them beyond what is a tolerable limit to them, watch out. They will explode. When they go, it is spectacular. Why is that? Because in their need for stability and acceptance, they often suppress personal frustrations. These can build up over time, until one day, under stress and pressure, these suppressed frustrations and emotions blow like a volcano.

You see how vital this skill of DISC rapport mastery is — to alter your DISC graphic equalisers to match those of others to meet their needs so they can stay on 16-cylinders, even under pressure.

Building rapport with more reserved high 'C's

Susan is reserved by nature and also more coolly task oriented in focus. She has a Conscientious or Cautious nature — a high 'C' graphic equaliser.

The high 'C's around you will bring great strength because they are so concerned with getting things right. They need detail, accuracy and quality and will work back late, even taking work home until the task is done 'right' to their own, self-imposed high standards.

The commitment to quality that people with a high 'C' Conscientious graphic equaliser like Susan bring to a team means they will often want more information.

Faced with a challenging situation, the active 'D' task people, like John in our example, will usually be keen to act. High 'C's like Susan will often argue, 'But we don't have enough information. To get this done well, we must do more market research.'

They are usually right, but you don't always have the time in rapidly changing environments to gather all the details. Sometimes, you must manage the enthusiasm of the active high 'D's and 'I's, and tackle the reticence of the more reserved nature of the high 'C's.

In establishing rapport with a high 'C', calm it down, be precise and specific.

High 'C' people, who are more reserved and task focused, need detail — so give it to them. If you yourself have a high 'I' graphic equaliser, the flexibility and energy required to build a rapport bridge to a slower paced, task oriented, high 'C' can be really challenging — but it is absolutely possible.

'C' under pressure

Under pressure, the high 'C's have a tendency to fall silent, because they have a deep need to be right and it is harder to be right in high pressure, fast changing environments. If you really pile up the pressure on a high 'C', they may withdraw. This is because it is easier to withdraw and remain right than it is to stay and argue — and risk the possibility of being wrong — which is their greatest fear.

So they usually fall silent and then leave — 'You lot simply don't know what you're talking about.' What will people do to get their needs met? Anything. So to stay right, the high 'C' withdraws.

▶ YOUR DISC GRAPHIC EQUALISER SETTINGS

Are you now clearer on your preferred DISC graphic equaliser settings? Are you by nature more people or more task focused, more active or more reserved? Where have you set your four DISC graphic equalisers?

This DISC rapport tool is a critical key to firing up 16-cylinder passion and performance in your team. If people will do anything to get their needs met, you have to make the right rapport choices and meet those needs. If people will do anything to avoid their fears — don't trigger their fears.

Make use of John Geier's outstanding tools for helping you analyse the DISC graphic equaliser settings of the people around you.

▶ RAPPORT FLEXIBILITY AND DISC MASTERY

It is impossible to attain mastery of rapport skills in a day, it takes practice. So you may wish to include this skill on your Commitments Register. If we are to play hard, I would suggest that mastering this skill is vital for tapping the hidden advantage in others.

Mastery of rapport implies having the maturity to meet others' needs instead of your own. For a high 'D' needing control, delegating a task to a team member can be extremely challenging. Because, while the employee has to get on with the task, the high 'D' manager has temporarily lost control, activating their fear button.

You can do this with each individual in the same meeting. The key is flexibility and moving your DISC graphic equalisers.

Top Tip: Slow down for the more reserved high 'S' and 'C' types of the team, to maintain their involvement. Speed up to keep the 'D' and 'I' types engaged. Your aim is to keep everyone fired up on 16-cylinders to achieve a vision and the results you are after.

To further enhance passion and enthusiasm, we will now explore a range of tools and approaches that speak directly to the spirit within the people around you.

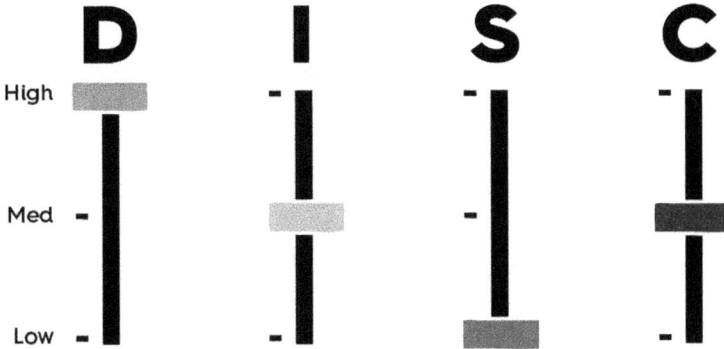

	D	**I**	**S**	**C**
High				
Med				
Low				

Dominant	High, Medium or Low?
Influencer	High, Medium or Low?
Steadiness	High, Medium or Low?
Conscientious	High, Medium or Low?

TEN

KEYS TO THE SPIRIT WITHIN

'I know of no single formula for success. But over the years I have observed that some attributes of leadership are universal and are often about finding ways of encouraging people to combine their efforts, their talents, their insights, their enthusiasm and their inspiration to work together.'
QUEEN ELIZABETH II

To build the rapport bridges, inspire your team's passion and enthusiasm, and to make sure they are totally motivated, you need to know how to directly address their 'en theos' — the spirit within.

Remember the word enthusiasm derives from the ancient Greek 'en theos' — the spirit within.

We have discussed that one key to enthusiasm is to ensure that the people around you have 'something significant yet to do'. They must have clear vision and know what their role is so they can justify the effort they are being asked to make.

Remember the spirit within is not looking for a job — the spirit within is looking for a game.

The most effective way to help people become motivated is to speak directly to their spirit. To give them a longer-term perspective on their life's journey, present them with a game — the $25 million dollar game.

▶ THE $25 MILLION GAME

There are two parts to the game, and it's specifically designed to help someone connect with their life purpose, what they came here to do. The clarity it provides extends far beyond their current role, occupation, or organisation.

The game can be a powerful experience — literally life-changing.

The game only works if approached with great personal honesty and courage. I invite you to take this opportunity and play the game.

Part One

Imagine yourself receiving a deposit of $25 million into your bank account.

This enables you to pay all your credit cards, mortgage etc. — all your debts. Or buy a home if you don't own one already.

Now you go out and buy $10 million worth of residential real estate to be rented out.

Assume you would receive a rental return of about 3 per cent. For the rest of your life, you would receive an income stream of about $300,000 a year and, as the years roll by, the rentals would increase in line with inflation.

The balance of the $25 million stays in your bank account.

The question for Part One of the game is then:

➡ **You now have an income stream of $300,000 a year and no debt. You live in a beautiful home. You do not have to 'work' anymore. What would you do with the rest of your life?**

For many people, this is a challenging question. Some people initially say, 'I don't know', or 'I would travel the world', or 'I would play golf every day'. As they think over the question, they write down all the things they would do if they did not have to exchange their time for money.

Let us assume that two years have gone by. If you were keen on travel, you've travelled the world — from the North Pole to the ice cliffs of Antarctica, from the great pyramid of Cheops to the Grand Canyon, from the Iguassu Falls in South America to the incredible lakes of Band-e-Amir in Afghanistan.

When you have done it all and seen it all, what are you going to do with the rest of your life?

The fascinating thing is that having played this game with thousands of people in hundreds of workshops around the world, over 90 per cent say they would like to spend time helping their fellow man or the planet — or both.

What they'd like as their epitaph — is that they made a difference.

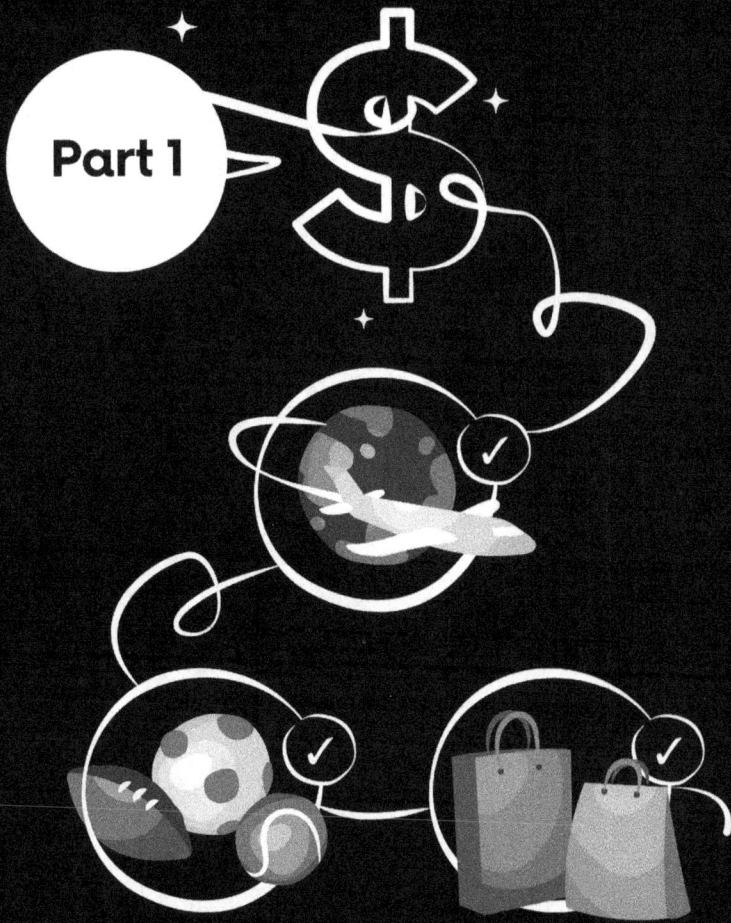

Part 1

You now have an income stream
of $300,000 a year and no debt.
You live in a beautiful home.
You do not have to 'work' anymore.
What would you do with the rest of your life?

Part 2

What is it that I am getting from working in this current "pottery" that is training me, developing me, stretching me, growing me for the bigger journey that lies ahead to achieve my life vision?

Not that they made sales quota or drove a Porsche or got to be General Manager. Why? Because this exercise speaks directly to the spirit within. And we have discussed that the spirit is not motivated by a job, the spirit is searching for a game – achieving life purpose.

'How strange is the lot of us mortals! Each of us here for a brief sojourn, for what purpose he knows not, though he senses it. But without deeper reflection one knows from daily life that one exists for other people.'
ALBERT EINSTEIN

Part Two

For most people, the money is most likely not out of the way. So, the second part of the exercise is to then ask a second question:

➡ **'From the first part of the game, you may have a better understanding of your longer term goals in life, possibly your life purpose. What are you receiving from the experiences and challenges in your current home and work environments that are training and preparing you for the achievement of your long term life goal or purpose?**

Part Two of the game demonstrates what you are gaining from your life roles at home and work.

Most people give a lot to their family life and their work. Recognise that. This game is about the balance of giving and receiving, the principle of exchange.

▶ SPIRIT EXCHANGE

For long-term motivation and enthusiasm, there must be a reasonable exchange between giving and receiving. This is a basic principle of spirit health.

Performance improvement means living in balance – giving and receiving.

When the spirit within is chronically out of balance, usually giving far more than receiving, enthusiasm dies and eventually the spirit disengages.

▶ SELF MOTIVATION

The principle behind the $25 million motivation game is simple.

If people have:

- ➡ **more clarity about their longer-term aims and life goals**
- ➡ **an understanding that life is a journey and achieving life purpose takes time and training**
- ➡ **a realisation that their role on your team has longer-term benefit and significance to their life journey**

Are they going to be more or less personally motivated when they wake up each morning?

Igniting someone's spirit is done by expanding their frame of reference to encompass their entire life journey. They can then assess this against their role today on your team and, if it's a win-win, they will be motivated to help you achieve your vision.

▶ LEADERSHIP STEWARDSHIP AND MENTORING

For all of us, our spirit within needs to be enthused.

The key to enthusing the spirit is to ensure there is a balance, an exchange of giving and receiving.

You want the people around you to give enthusiastically so you can achieve your vision, but are they receiving in return? What are you giving them for their life journey?

As a leader, you have a mentoring responsibility to the people around you.

At a deep spirit level, your fundamental responsibility as a leader is to ensure that the people under your care gain the skills they'll need to achieve their life vision.

At a deep spirit level, the purpose of any enterprise is for the people around you to develop metaphysical 'muscles' by working on and solving home, community and work challenges — and growing through the process.

'If you want to go fast, go alone. If you want to go far, go together.'
AFRICAN PROVERB.

A PERSONAL GROWTH CONTRACT

Consider developing a personal growth contract with each of your people to clarify their life paths. Your contribution to their personal growth will maximise their enthusiasm.

The chances are that they will have never experienced this with any other organisation. Once they can see there is a healthy spirit exchange, and that you are concerned about their longer-term life journey, then their spirit passion will fire up.

If people are off track, they will know it at some deep level. They may not have had the clarity to face it without the $25 million game, but they will know. They may have been going through the motions for years on about five cylinders. They lose, you lose.

Once people have played the $25 million game, they have three choices:

1. **See their role in a new light and fire up.**

2. **See they have stopped growing in their current role and either re-define that role or seek an expanded role.**

3. **Leave and find a new role and a new training challenge which opens up a vacancy for the 'right' journeyman on your team.**

One of the toughest jobs of leadership, as we run 21st century companies with flat organisation structures, is to see bright young people leave and move on because we can't expand fast enough to keep them challenged by our organisation. But they leave with our blessing. If we all understand the life journey metaphor, they can always come back in the future, if the right opportunity appears, with a whole new set of skills and experiences that can help us achieve our vision.

Some organisation's view leaving as an act of betrayal and would never consider that person returning. That is an interesting stance. A master craftsman would always welcome back a high performing journeyman to help the team. Time away on the journey can only have enhanced the breadth and depth of experience.

If someone shares that they are not enjoying anything like the balance they are looking for, and they are leaving your organisation, then counsel them to review the opportunities on your team before they leave. Maybe they are not seeing the areas from which they are gaining growth. Could it be that an internal transfer within your organisation could be what they need? Explore all options.

However, if they see they cannot achieve that balance on your team, then they must leave. Let them go in search of a team that gives them a renewed sense of balance and the personal growth they need.

Is someone on the production line, who says they work a shift just for the money, going to relate to this approach? Possibly not. But everyone has a spirit within. It's just that many people have shut their spirit down, surviving life on three or four cylinders. Sure, they do a passable job. Your challenge is to fire them up, even the 'shut down' ones, on 16-cylinders using these passion tools.

You can't afford to have five-cylinder passengers in a 21st century business. So, turn them on or out.

▶ THE DOMAINS OF BALANCE

Not everyone has the same goals. Most people around you are working for money as part of the 'contract'. But money is not everything and people have different areas of focus and priorities.

The following model may help you — and them — understand their priorities, enabling you to fire up their spirit being.

The model is called the domains of balance and is this — our life is focused across several areas of responsibility and interests. Life can place us under tremendous pressure and stress. However, for long-term health, there must be a balance between the different areas of our life. These domains have a logical sequence or hierarchy, although we may individually place differing emphasis on individual domains.

Understanding the importance of these domains to the people around you provides another spirit passion key.

First domain — Self

The first domain is your true self, the essence of you, your Spirit Being. You are the most important person in your life. You must look after the interests of your spirit within. For optimum motivation, the spirit must be in exchange with a balance of giving and receiving.

7 Domains

7D **Metaphysical World**
Great spirit, universal intelligence,
God, Allah, Brahma, Jehovah

6D **Physical World**
MEST - matter, energy, space and time

5D **Body & Environment**
Living Beings

4D **Humanity**
Wider Community

3D **Teams**
Work

2D **Relationships**
Close relationships & Family

1D **Self**
Spirit

You are no use to anyone else if you are shut down at the spirit level, just going through the motions. You must be clear what you need for spirit health. You already have guidelines from our review of clear vision and something significant yet to do.

Second domain — Relationships

The second domain is your close relationships. You are no use to your family and close friends if you are sick, miserable, or depressed with your spirit shut down. So, your spirit comes first. However, life on your own can be lonely. Looking after family and close relationships is the second important part of a balanced life.

The challenge is significant, but the second domain is a powerful motivator and a source of significant passion.

Third domain — Teams

The first domain and priority is to look after ourselves, our own Spirit Being. The second priority and responsibility is to our family and close relationships. Work and business teams take third place. You are no use at work if your first and second domains are chronically out of balance.

For long-term 16-cylinder performance, you need to respect the balance and priorities of these first three domains.

We have to emphasise the word 'domain' because life can go out of balance in the short term. Sometimes we have to go away on business for a month or work the next five weekends. Or our daughter breaks her ankle playing soccer and we need to take some time off to look after her or start work later than usual.

Life is life. Aim for balance.

Fourth domain — Humanity

The fourth domain is the wider community and humanity. Some people spend significant time helping their community. It could be coaching your child's sport team or helping a local charity. It is impossible to contribute to the community if you are dis-spirited and down, your family life is a mess, and you are out of work. Which is why the wider community and humanity is ranked fourth.

By showing sincere interest and building rapport with the people around you, you can help them to optimise their contribution to the wider community and thus increase their motivation and passion.

Fifth domain — Body & Environment

The fifth domain covers the physical aspects of life — our bodies and planet Earth. We need to care for our bodies and we need to do our bit for the planet — and all living things.

You need to recognise and respect other people's interests and incorporate those into your dealings with them when building rapport and motivating them.

Sixth domain — Physical World

The sixth domain is our physical universe of matter, energy, space, and time. This is the realm of the houses, the toys, the cars, the boats, the ski trips and travel.

The sixth domain is the realm of money and finance. Clearly, for most people, the sixth domain is very important.

Seventh domain — Metaphysical World

The seventh domain of the Metaphysical World is the unseen realm of spirit being consciousness, thought, ethics and morals.

The seventh domain also includes what the North American Indians call 'Great Spirit'.

Others speak of God, Allah, Brahma, Jehovah, Universal Intelligence or Source. It is the spiritual domain. In the seventh domain, the choices people make in how they relate to 'higher intelligence', is often very private and not open to public debate.

Devout Christians may object to swearing in the workplace. Working on the Sabbath for some people is untenable. Observing the dawn to dusk fast during Ramadan is tough going. Doing challenging mental work on late afternoon low blood sugar is not easy for a whole month. Respect people's seventh domain beliefs.

They are generally not open to debate and are trashed at your peril. Discreetly supported, they can be tremendous spirit motivators.

The domains of balance as motivators

You should find out which domains are most important to each person around you.

Is it that by working harder, with more passion, they can earn more money on the sixth domain?

Is it that their true passion is for their family and that the rewards from working hard, reflect as a better family lifestyle?

Or could it be that they value the part-time nature of their employment because they wish to contribute to the wider community?

You are looking to turn on long-term passion. Understanding what is important to each person you interact with gives you a powerful tool for making it crystal clear what they have to gain from being involved with you.

A further source of passion and strength derives from people's values and beliefs. We will now explore additions to the range of passion keys you have at your disposal.

'Alone we can do so little; together we can do so much.'
HELEN KELLER

Geier explained
that our behaviours
are influenced by
three major areas:

Behaviour

Thoughts & feelings

Values & beliefs

Needs & fears

ELEVEN

VALUES A SOURCE OF STRENGTH

'The way is not in the sky; the way is in the heart.'
GAUTAMA BUDDHA

You have, by now, mapped the territory, achieved rapport, catered to people's deep needs, and inspired their 'en theos' — the spirit within.

Let us re-visit the iceberg model of why people behave as they do. Let's focus on people's values and beliefs which provides yet another tool to get them firing on all 16-cylinders.

▶ THE DOMAINS OF BALANCE

Our thoughts and feelings, and therefore our behaviours, are strongly influenced by our values and beliefs.

A belief is an idea or concept we trust, accept, and easily understand.

Not everyone's beliefs are the same, and they can be contradictory.

Christopher Columbus believed the world was round when many of his crew still believed the world was flat. Therefore, his thoughts and feelings about sailing west across the Atlantic differed from his crew. Without his beliefs, their beliefs and fears about falling off the edge of the world, would have caused them to turn the ship around and sail back home to Spain.

The word value derives from the Latin verb 'valere' — to be strong.

But what is a value?

A value is very important to us, something worth standing up for, something that gives our life meaning. Values influence behaviour. We can understand someone's behaviour by seeking to understand their values.

I have known people with strong religious beliefs unable to attend weekend workshops on their day of worship, even though they were keen to participate and contribute.

We must respect other people's values even if we don't understand or agree with them. If you can understand and respect other people's values, you hold another powerful key to firing up their 16-cylinders of passion and enthusiasm.

▶ VALUES AND BEHAVIOUR ARE CIRCUMSTANCE RELATED

Value driven behaviour can be frustrating and difficult to understand and deal with. This is because values can depend on circumstances and can change as those circumstances change.

Imagine a very large bowl full of horrible, brown, live cockroaches. The bowl is squirming with them.

In normal circumstances would you eat this bowl of live cockroaches for five dollars? Most people would say — 'You must be joking!'

Would you eat a large bowl of live cockroaches for 1,000 dollars? You would still probably answer 'No.'

What about for 100,000 dollars or one million dollars? Would you eat a big bowl of live cockroaches for 100 million dollars?

Some people might eat a bowl of live cockroaches for $100,000 and some people would not consider it for 100 million dollars. They have strong value judgments on what they will and won't eat.

But imagine this next scenario. You have spent the last five years in solitary confinement. You are a hair's breadth away from death due to starvation. You know that you will be released in two weeks' time — if you can stay alive. Would you change your normal behaviour and eat the cockroaches?

Most people answer, 'Of course, I would do anything to stay alive.'

Values give us strength. But values can also be malleable and loaded with emotions and change according to circumstances.

What gives your life meaning and influences your behaviour in 'normal' situations could be entirely different if you found yourself in the jungle, being hunted by a hostile force or separated from your family and friends.

Yet values can be very powerful motivators and need to be elicited and understood to optimise rapport.

▶ UNDERSTANDING THE VALUES OF OTHER PEOPLE

If you can understand and respect other people's values, you have another powerful key to fire up their passion and enthusiasm. This is because people usually feel strongly about the values they hold.

Although values are powerful, they can be hard to elicit because they potentially operate below normal conscious awareness. The best way to elicit someone's values is to ask them what gives their life meaning.

People can list a wide variety of possible answers to what gives their life meaning — family, relationships, love, understanding, recognition, work, giving, spirit integrity, honesty, fitness, respect, caring, money, possessions, hobbies, helping other people, freedom, health, friends, career, being of service, security, quality, challenge, growth, contribution, travel, learning, religion. The list is as variable as the people that write them and can cover all seven domains.

However everyone, given ten minutes, can produce a personal list of what gives their life meaning. It takes a bit of time because some values are deep and usually under conscious awareness until we stop and think about them. Try making your list.

Then rank the value list by numbering each value on the list according to importance. Then re-write the list of the top 5 values from 1 to 5.

➡ **1. First most important value** _____

➡ **2. Second most important value** _____

➡ **3. Third most important value** _____

➡ **4. Fourth most important value** _____

➡ **5. Fifth most important value** _____

Then test the relative importance of each value by starting at the bottom of the list and asking:

- ➡ **If I had value 4 but not value 5 is that okay?**
- ➡ **If it is not okay, then reverse the order to ascertain the sequence of personal importance:**
- ➡ **If I had value 5 and not value 4 is that okay?**
- ➡ **If that feels right then re-number values 4 and 5. If that feels okay, then go up to the next pair and test again:**
- ➡ **If I had value 3 and not value 4 is that okay?**
- ➡ **Then proceed to test up the value list.**
- ➡ **This tool helps people to clarify their number one value. This is what they are striving for in life.**
- ➡ **Knowing this gives them, and you, a profound key to fire up their inner strength, passion and drives — especially relevant in turbulent and challenging times.**
- ➡ **What's your number one value? What you are striving for? Does it give your life meaning at a deep spirit level?**

▶ COMPANY VALUE STATEMENTS

People are motivated by a myriad of different values and that makes finding common ground, in any group of people, a challenge.

Try to find a common set of values — but just know they will end up as general guidelines. They will not appeal to everyone involved, nevertheless, they will be useful to have.

▶ SUMMARY

Over the last few chapters, we have explored tools and approaches to build rapport bridges with the people around you. We have reviewed a range of tools to fire up people's passion by recognising and respecting:

- ➡ **Their DISC profile (needs and fears)**
- ➡ **Their Spirit Being**
- ➡ **Their values**

You now have the tools to adjust your rapport approaches and be flexible to match people's needs in all these areas.

You will build these rapport bridges, mostly, below their conscious awareness. In some regards, you are a different person for each person around you because you are striving to achieve mastery across that bridge of rapport.

You need not master these tools all simultaneously. The goal of being skilled enough to inspire passion, enthusiasm and 16-cylinder performance in the people around you is a vital demonstration of life journey skills mastery and essential for accessing the hidden advantage latent in others.

Mastery is a life long journey. You may have heard the quote attributed to the ancient Chinese philosopher, Lao-Tzu:

'The journey of a thousand miles begins with the first step.'

Don't feel overwhelmed. Take one tool at a time and practice it for a month or so. Consider committing to mastery of the tools as a life-long journey and goal — if you are serious about empowering and inspiring other people.

Our discussion on passion, however, cannot rest here. That is because, as soon as you have two or more people working together, you enter the domain of team culture.

We are all involved with a group of people at home, in our community or at work. Developing high performance teams is a vital skill because you can rarely achieve your vision on your own.

How do you want your team to play the game? How do you want them to work together to achieve the vision?

Let's explore!

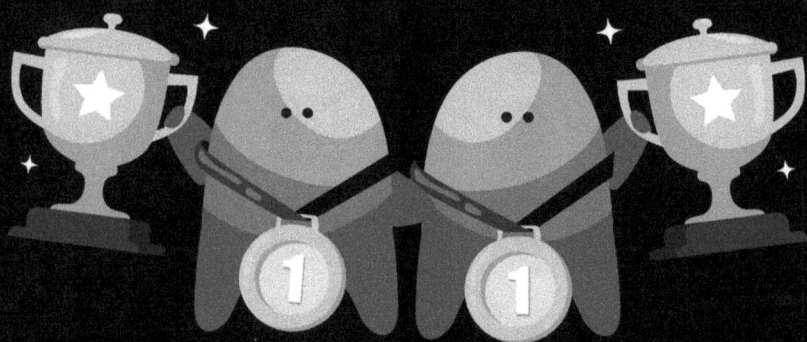

TWELVE

BUILDING PASSIONATE TEAMS

'Employees who believe that management is concerned about them as a whole person — not just an employee — are more productive, more satisfied, more fulfilled. Satisfied employees mean satisfied customers, which leads to profitability.'

ANNE M. MULCAHY — CEO XEROX

The word culture is derived the Latin noun 'cultus' — care.

Now that you have the tools to inspire the individual passions of people around you, you have to fire them up and motivate them as a team. The key is team culture.

How do you want the team to work together to achieve the vision? How do you want to care for your team?

▶ TEAM CULTURE

There are two crucial keys that define the culture of a team that we will cover to ensure you have the tools to develop and sustain a culture of success.

The two keys to a success culture are:

1. **Trust**

2. **Assertion**

Let's now review the keys to trust and assertion and how to apply them to unlock team passion and performance. This will help you to maximise harmony and performance at home, in your organisation and in your community.

▶ TRUST AND ASSERTION

The culture of a team is strongly influenced by how much trust is present between the people on the team, and how much assertion is evident from the people, especially when problems arise.

Both trust and assertion are essential for long-term, 16-cylinder team performance. We will now explore some practical tools to help you and your team with these team passion keys.

The diagram shown here has four quadrants for four different approaches to team culture. Each needs to be explored to consider the ramifications.

Low trust/low assertion = lose/lose

If there is little trust amongst the team members and not enough assertion — then the culture spirals down. It's lose/lose.

Lose/lose means just that. The people 'turn off' and their passion cylinders shut down. The organisation also loses out because it is not getting the benefit of a switched on, passionate team. So, everyone loses.

High assertion/low trust = win/lose

If there is strong assertion and very little trust, you enter the domain of dog eat dog, the strong and powerful dominate and the team game is win/lose. I win because I play hard — and you lose. Nice guys finish last.

There are two reasons why you cannot allow loud, aggressive people to dominate a team with their win/lose tactics.

First is Team: Together Everyone Achieves More.

Second: The more reserved people have the higher acuity; they see more detail. If you let the strong and powerful assert all the time, the reserved people will fall silent, and you and the team will lose their valuable insights.

There is nothing wrong with assertion, it is an essential skill of high-performance teams. What you need though is a practical tool for assertion that will 'level the playing field' and give the more reserved people on the team an equal voice.

High trust/low assertion = lose/win

Out there in the real world of life and business, there are the win/lose sharks waiting to take you out as shark bait. So, where there is very little assertion, not enough ability to confront conflict or speak up on the real issues that are not being addressed, everyone ends up being too nice. 'NICE' is an acronym:

➡ **Nothing Inside me Cares Enough**

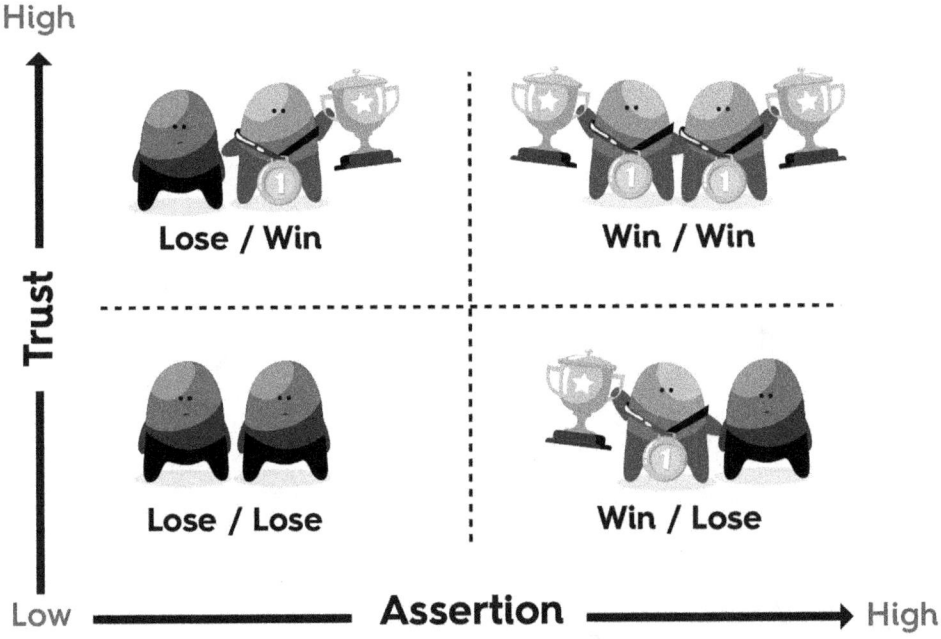

High

Trust

Low   Assertion   High

Lose / Win   Win / Win

Lose / Lose   Win / Lose

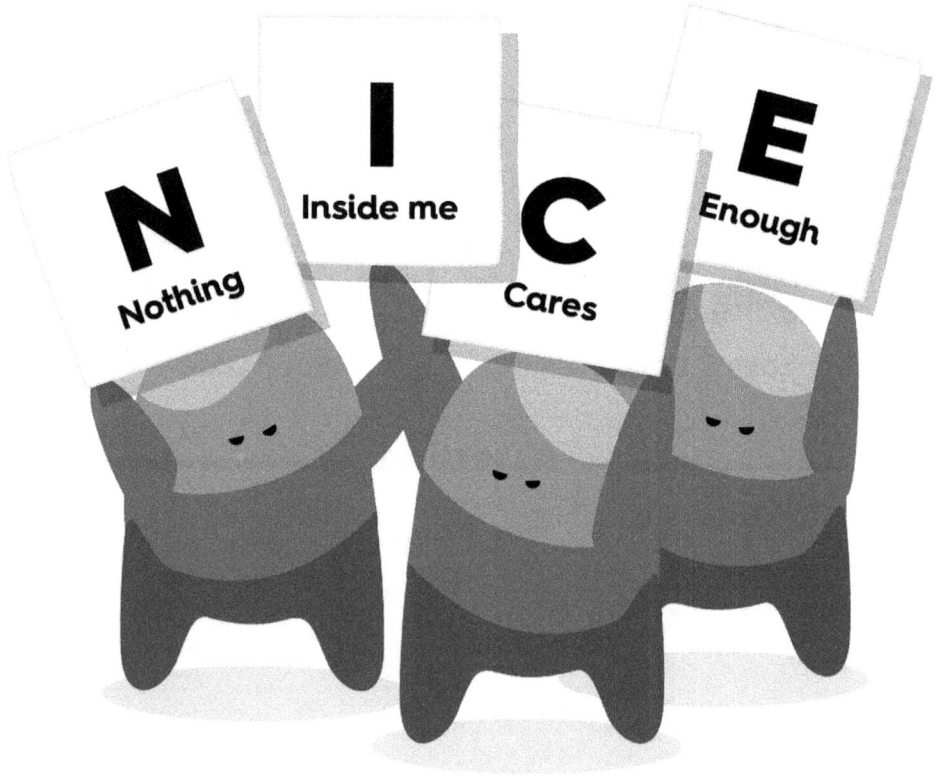

Where there is a high level of trust, where everyone is 'nice', when no one has enough courage or assertion to speak up, then your team can descend into the dreadful domain of lose/win. The win/lose sharks are assertive, they couldn't care less about trust, they have a winner takes all attitude and who is taken out as shark bait? YOU.

So, win/lose means the aggressors win — and the meek, trusting team loses. You've probably seen that amusing graffiti: The meek shall inherit the earth... if that's all right with you!

Clearly many people adopt a win/lose approach to life. Life journey skills mastery, however, demands a more fulfilling, yet harder to achieve, approach to developing and sustaining team culture — win/win.

High trust/high assertion = win/win

If you are to create a resilient culture that is also fun, empowering, fulfilling and rewarding — the 16-cylinder environment — you need both trust and assertion.

To ensure you have a passionate team, a team that is operating at full power through thick and thin, it is important that we review both axes — trust and assertion — and equip you with practical tools for both skills.

Trust

Let us first review trust. Why is it that — in the pressured games of life and business — there is often not a great deal of trust evident?

▶ OUR WIN/LOSE HISTORY

Look at our history. Where were our ancestors living 2.5 million years ago — from the time archaeologists found fossilised remains of primitive man in the Olduvai Gorge in Tanzania?

Our ancestors were living in caves playing the game of survival.

When lunch came onto the plain, if Cave Family 'A' were slow off the mark and Cave Family 'B' grabbed lunch first — Cave Family 'A' starved.

There wasn't always enough food to go around and so our ancestors often found themselves living in a world of scarcity, a world of win/lose. The fundamental lesson was — grab it while you can.

The game of win/lose, 'grab it while you can' or 'grab as much as you can' has been in our genes for millions of years.

Under pressure, most people immediately slip into win/lose behaviour. They play it safe. That could be assessed as a sensible strategy. If it looks like there is going to be a loser here, rather you than me!

▶ TRUST BUILDING TOOLS

What can you do to encourage and build trust on a team with 2.5 million years of conditioning stacked against you? Remember, a team has to produce outstanding performance when the heat is on — and disagreement about alternative action options is a real possibility.

In Chapter 9 on rapport, we reviewed the four behaviours of trust — reliability, openness, acceptance, and straightforwardness.

Clearly, demonstrating those behaviours yourself — and expecting those behaviours from your team — is a start.

The Trust Account

To help you build trust, a useful tool is the concept of 'the trust account'.

Let's use the analogy of a bank account as we're all familiar with those. You put money in (deposits), and you take money out (withdrawals).

If you deposit more than you withdraw, you build a positive bank balance. What happens to your bank account if you start making more withdrawals than deposits? Your bank balance goes down. If you persist in this behaviour, it goes down to zero. If you persist further in taking out more than you put in, you become overdrawn.

On any team, there is an equivalent concept called 'the trust account'. It is intangible but everybody on the team instinctively knows the trust balance of the team's trust account.

Trust account deposits

To achieve a positive, 16-cylinder team culture, you need a positive trust account balance. How do you build up a positive trust account balance?

Family
A

Family
B

2.5 Million BC

Scarcity grab as much as you can! Win/ Lose

Deposit

Trust

Account

Withdrawal

By making trust deposits.

By ensuring that your trust behaviours are consistent. By ensuring that your team members are aware of, and agree to, the need for the same trust behaviours.

By making agreements with each other and keeping them.

By ensuring that you and your team all use the passion tools that we have reviewed to respect and nurture:

➡ **each other's DISC needs**

➡ **the en theos — their spirit within**

➡ **each other's values**

➡ **each other's domains of balance**

By aiming for improved understanding and frequent, high-quality communication between team members.

Trust account withdrawals

Why are trust deposits so important?

Because, for every team, there are going to be trust withdrawals — called mistakes. They are inevitable.

Remember the two teams — the winning team and the learning team. How does the learning team learn? By making lots of mistakes. So, mistakes are inevitable. Even the more reserved, task focused high 'C' Conscientious people with their need to get it right sometimes get it wrong.

If a team has built up a strong, positive trust balance in the team's invisible trust account, the team can handle an inevitable, occasional mistake — a trust withdrawal. The team will rally round, solve the mistake, and use the mistake to increase trust deposits in the future through organisational learning.

However, if you make more trust withdrawals than trust deposits, the trust balance goes down until it reaches zero. The result? A demoralised team.

What are you going to do to build up the trust account on your team? As mistakes are bound to happen, it could be time to re-visit your Commitments Register and note down some specific trust deposit actions.

▶ ASSERTION

Having devised strategies to improve your team's ability to establish and maintain trust and cooperation, we now need to review the second crucial aspect of team culture — assertion.

In many organisations, people are 'too nice' to speak up and address the real issues that should be confronted for success to be assured.

The challenge is to be able to assert ourselves and our views clearly — without becoming rude or aggressive.

This is definitely a challenge. Well-meant assertion by more active people can be perceived as aggression by more reserved people.

You need an assertion tool that everyone on your team can use — irrespective of their personality type.

An assertion tool

The following icon represents one of the best assertion tools.

You can see the icon has two big eyes, two big ears and how many mouths? None. That's a clue! The words that accompany this icon are 'I feel like saying'. It is a powerful tool of assertion.

The rule of the assertion tool is that, In a team meeting, if somebody says 'I feel like saying', then everybody else shuts up and listens to what the person has to say.

Why do you need an assertion tool? Because, as we've seen, the more active people with high 'D' and 'I' DISC graphic equalisers (with a need for control and recognition) can dominate the conversation. Not that they mean to undermine anyone, it's just how they operate.

What then happens to all that valuable input from the more reserved personality types? You won't have access to it when you need it most.

Remember. They have higher acuity. They see solutions that others miss. The problem is that they are more reserved by nature so they will not speak up, especially when conflict presents. If you allow this to happen, then your choices will be sub-optimal.

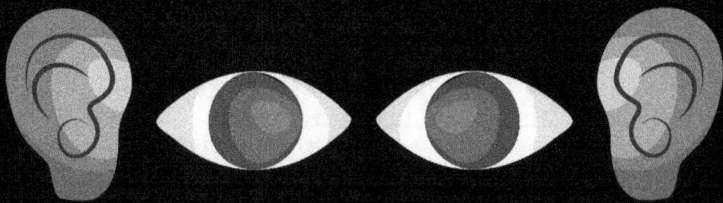

Assertion Tool

I feel like saying

▶ CONFLICT

Remember what they say about conflict — if two people always agree on everything, one of them is not necessary! Conflict is healthy. You need conflict in your team if you are going to achieve gold standard results.

If you place iron ore and coking coal in a crucible, and warm it with a candle for several hours, you will end up with warm iron ore and coking coal. However, if you replace the candle with a white hot flame, you produce steel.

It is the same with developing vision, plans and team culture.

You sometimes need the white hot heat of conflict and disagreement to hone steel-like responses and action plans from your team.

▶ I FEEL LIKE SAYING

The 'I feel like saying' tool engenders balance.

It gives everybody a chance to assert their ideas in a non-aggressive way. Once the 'I feel like saying' words have been spoken, everybody else shuts up and listens.

The assertion tool is easy to introduce to your team. It is a great equaliser of rank, providing that the tool is respected. It needs explanation and practice like any other new tool.

A word of caution — you can easily misuse the 'I feel like saying' tool.

If you use the tool to open up a space for team dialogue and are then rude or personal with people on your team, you can destroy the tool forever. No-one will respect or trust it again.

Other uses for the 'I feel like saying' tool

The 'I feel like saying' assertion tool has other uses. You can use it at the start of a meeting.

Even though people are physically present in a meeting, their minds might still grapple with yesterday's problems, or worrying about tomorrow's problems, — they are not really 'present' in the room. So, one of the uses for 'I feel like saying' is to start a meeting by going around the team and inviting them to say 'what they feel like saying'. It is a great tool to focus attention on the meeting and ensure that you have a quality meeting.

▶ RITUALS

Using the tool like this becomes a ritual. Rituals are important to any tribe or society. Rituals are the glue that binds the culture of the team. Using 'I feel like saying' is a great ritual.

You can also close your meetings with the 'I feel like saying' tool. It becomes another ritual. It can give everyone a final voice letting everyone leave the meeting feeling heard. You could ask the team to close with a positive statement that includes a personal commitment to action.

The tool encourages each of the team to clarify their summation thoughts before leaving the meeting.

▶ SUMMARY

Now you have a vision — preferably co-created with other people.

You also have keys to understand both your own sources of passion and those of the people around you. Everybody on your team is different. You have to ensure each team member is firing on all 16-cylinders, with a burning desire to succeed and enough passion to optimise your chances of success.

However, any team with a powerful vision, fired up with maximum enthusiasm and passion, is not going to get very far unless you have the third success key from Think and Grow Rich — clear plans of action.

PART FOUR:
PLANNING

THIRTEEN

CLEAR PLANS OF ACTION

'It takes as much energy to wish as it does to plan.'
ELEANOR ROOSEVELT

▶ MAKING IT HAPPEN

The world is dangerously full of spectators and gonna do's.

Spectators are at their best at football matches. Screaming advice and comments at the players and abusing the ref. If they were really that good, how come they are not down on the pitch playing the game?

It's the same in the game of life and business. If you create a challenging vision and game plan for your life and your business, the spectators will undoubtedly show up to critique your performance and explain where you are going wrong.

Gonna do's are the ones with the dreams but no action.

To live your life with passion and enthusiasm demands that you must have clear plans of action.

The third success key is developing clear plans of action. Note there are two parts — plans and action. You have to plan and then act.

The challenge of planning is finding the time required to do it as we all seem to be constantly pressured by urgent matters that have to be handled.

You know that plans are important but, as they are not always urgent, they can be relegated to 'tomorrow'.

Carving out quality time for planning is a discipline you and your team must master if you are to produce excellent results.

Most organisations seem to operate in a consistent culture of urgency. Without plans, you can't tell which urgent matters are important and which are, in reality, not that important.

Good planning is a vital tool.

▶ PLANNING TRAPS

There are three planning traps to be aware of.

Let's cover them now so you and your team can avoid them.

Planning trap number one — Fear of the future

The first trap of planning is fear of the future. People find looking ahead to be challenging. They prefer to focus on living in the now.

Because most people seem to have a deep-seated, usually unarticulated fear of the future, you must have a planning method that avoids this first planning trap.

Planning trap number two — What's the next step?

The second trap of planning is slightly more insidious.

Let us assume that you have, along with your team, overcome any fear of the future and co-created a powerful vision of your team's future.

You stand now in present time, looking into the future at your inspiring vision.

Somebody then asks the wrong question — 'What's the next step?' The second trap of planning.

'What's the next step?' Why is that the wrong question?

Because if you have intelligent people on your team, they will all come up with plenty of good ideas on the next step on your team's journey to achieving the vision.

The issue is that all of their ideas have a little bit of personal 'ego' attached to them.

Everyone will have a slightly different view of what to do. The end result can be that everyone wants to head off in different directions.

To succeed you need a set of plans and laser beam focus.

The planning tool in this chapter neatly avoids the planning trap of 'what's the next step?'

Planning trap number three — The Merlin factor

Merlin was the wizard at King Arthur's court and this third planning trap is known as the Merlin factor.

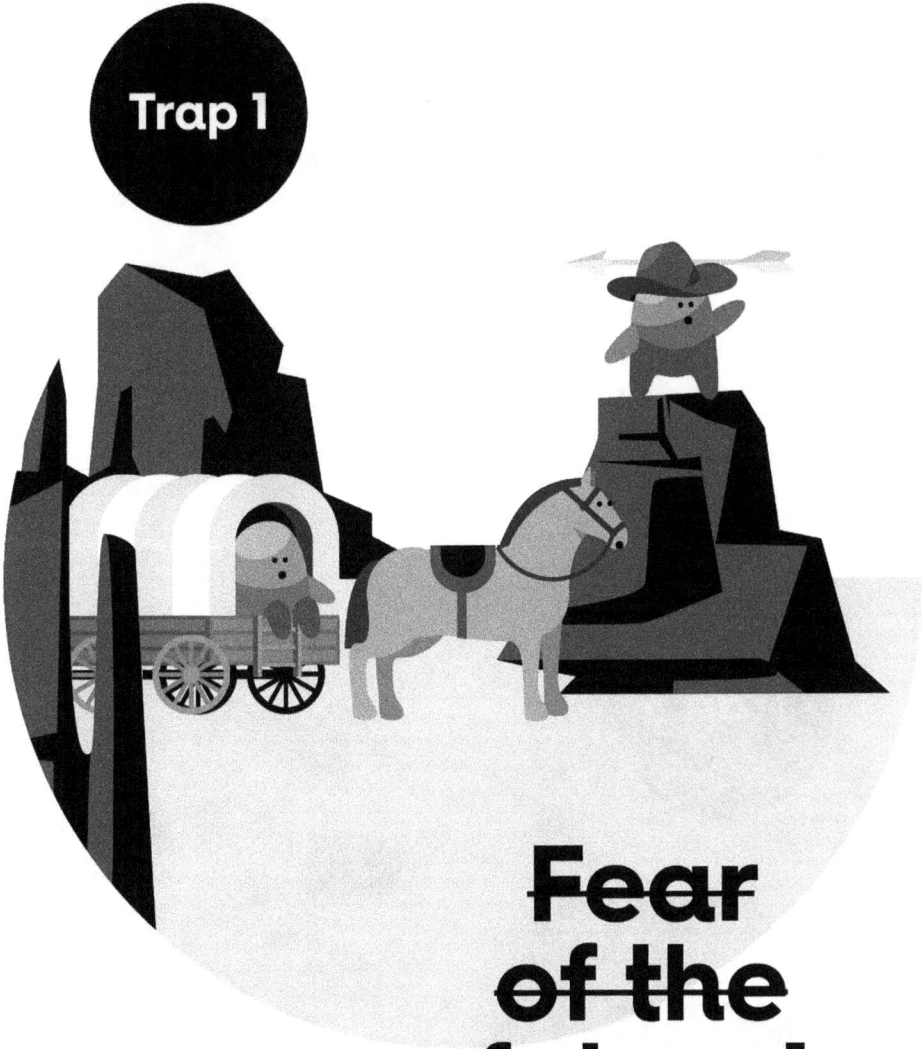

Trap 1

Fear
of the
future!

Trap 2

~~What's the next step?~~

Trap 3

~~That won't work!~~

Merlin explained to King Arthur's knights that the reason he was so wise was that he could see into the future.

He further explained, there was something that made it very difficult for the knights as they struggled forward in present time. Not only were they not able to see into the future, but they were also dragging something heavy behind them — the past.

We are all dragging our past behind us, and the third trap of planning shows up in the phrase 'that won't work!'

Your team wants to move forward towards a vision with plans of action. Someone comes up with a good idea of what to do next. You can't see into the future to know if the idea will work. However, your team has lots of past experiences from their journeys through life so it's easy for someone to say — 'No, that won't work' and then give good reasons from the past to explain why.

No one on the team knows whether that judgement is justified or not, but the idea is crushed anyway. I'm sure you've experienced this in meetings. Good ideas are rejected before they are given a chance. This is a serious planning trap that can erode enthusiasm by reducing choices — and you need to avoid it.

Quality planning

If you are to succeed in firing up the 16-cylinders of each individual on your team, you have to have a planning methodology that avoids these three traps of planning:-

1. **Fear of the future — 'Let's just focus on today.'**

2. **The wrong question — 'What's the next step?'**

3. **The Merlin factor — 'That won't work.'**

The planning solution

Fortunately, this challenge of avoiding the three planning traps has been solved for all of us.

There is a great story told by fellow trainer and facilitator, Blair Singer.

The story describes the origins of a powerful planning tool that will allow you to produce outstanding, clear plans of action.

In 1961, President John. F. Kennedy went on world radio and television and announced to the world that his nation would put a man on the moon by the end of the decade. The problem was that John F. Kennedy did not know how to build a rocket to take the Americans to the moon.

At the time of Kennedy's announcement, one of the senior men on the American space program was Wernher von Braun. Wernher was Director of Development Operations for NASA, and, during the second world war, he had been one of Germany's top rocket scientists.

When it came to rockets and space flight, Wernher knew his stuff. So, after Kennedy's speech, Wernher contacted the White House staff and suggested the President went back onto world television to explain that he was only kidding.

Reaching the moon by the end of the decade was impossible. It couldn't be done! The White House staff told him, in no uncertain terms, that the challenge lay with him and his colleagues.

The US Navy Special Projects office came to Wernher's rescue.

After the war, it was very clear that not only were rockets and missiles going to be important, but if you had your rockets on land, they would also be sitting ducks for the enemy. It was necessary to have the rockets moving around on the water or better still, under the water. So, in 1958, the navy formed the Polaris Weapons System Program — with the highest military priority.

In developing Polaris, they developed a powerful new planning methodology.

The Navy told Wernher that to succeed, he had to avoid the three traps of planning. To do this, he had to go forward into the future. The Americans will be on the moon by the end of the decade, the President has said so.

The second planning trap for Wernher to avoid was for him to ensure that he and his team did not ask the wrong question — 'what's the next step?' As the team members probably all had IQs of 160+, he would have hundreds, if not thousands of bright ideas, all with a little bit of 'ego' attached to them, all potentially heading off in different directions.

P E R T

Program   Evaluation   Review   Technique

Thirdly, he had to be careful to avoid the Merlin factor cutting in — 'That won't work'.

The navy explained to Wernher that his planning approach had to be to work back from the desired future, from NASA's vision of success (a man on the moon), by asking one question repeatedly:

'What happened just before that?'

The planning methodology called PERT — Program Evaluation and Review Technique — was born.

Clearly, we are all faced with multiple possible futures. A graphical vision enables us to choose our desired future. The PERT planning tool allows us to work back from that envisioned success.

This is vital when linked with the reality creation tools used with the deeper parts of the mind. We'll cover this in Chapter 14 on the power of the mind.

▶ PERT EXPLAINED

The PERT planning method is a very simple yet powerful tool. It requires you to start with the end in mind — with your vision of success — and then work back to the present time by continually asking that one question:

'What happened just before that?'

Example — The Apollo mission

As an example of the PERT planning process in action, let's review the case of the American moon landing. The future, success vision was Neil Armstrong standing on the surface of the moon.

What did he say on that momentous occasion on July 20th, 1969 — 'That's one small step for man, one giant leap for mankind.'

With Neil Armstrong standing on the moon, the PERT planning tool demands one question:

'What happened just before that?'

The ladder was lowered by the lunar lander, the Eagle, to the lunar surface.

'What happened just before that?'

The Eagle landed.

'What happened just before that?'

The Eagle undocked from the Apollo capsule orbiting the moon.

'What happened just before that?'

The Apollo craft went into orbit around the moon.

'What happened just before that?'

Mid-course correction.

'What happened just before that?'

Blast-off from Cape Kennedy.

The PERT planning tool works from an agreed future vision, planning in incremental steps, back through time.

Was NASA's ultimate goal to have a man standing on the moon? No.

The ultimate goal was to have the astronauts safely back on the deck of the aircraft carrier in the South Pacific.

The astronauts are on the deck of the carrier.

'What happened just before that?'

The astronauts are retrieved from the capsule, floating in the sea.

'What happened just before that?'

Splash down.

'What happened just before that?'

Main parachutes open.

'What happened just before that?'

Re-entry.

'What happened just before that?'

All the way back from the moon,

PERT planning is effective

As a planning tool, PERT is effective because it avoids the three traps of planning:

1. **Fear of the future.**

2. **'What's the next step?'**

3. **The Merlin Factor — 'That won't work.'**

Working back from an agreed future vision is a positive experience and leaves no room for negativity. Try the technique for yourself. My experience with clients all over the world has shown PERT to be a very powerful tool for making better decisions, and better choices, as you plan back from your vision.

As time goes by, the external environment can throw up unforeseen challenges. The opposition is always strategising.

When the unexpected occurs — as it will — the first question to ask is, does the vision have to change? If so, change it. If not, do the current plans need modification, given the new challenges? If so, then start with the agreed vision and plan back through the new challenges to avoid falling into the three planning traps we have discussed.

▶ PERT AS A GRAPHICAL PLANNING TECHNIQUE

A graphical vision, supported by the PERT planning tool, is a powerful combination. Why? Because it involves all three (VAK) senses and produces goals that are visually striking along with clear plans.

Again, a picture (graphical plans) is worth a thousand words (written plans).

Let me explain the process.

You will need to set up large sheets of white paper on the wall and then give your team members post-it notes and pens.

PERT is a planning language based upon two components, events, and relationships. It is easy to learn and use.

▶ EVENTS

An event occurs at a specific point in time and is described by a noun (a thing) and a verb (an action). Let's clarify this with some examples:

➡ **Event = Mount Everest Conquered**

➡ **Noun = Mount Everest**

➡ **Verb = Conquered**

EVENT

=

NOUN
Thing

+

VERB
an Action

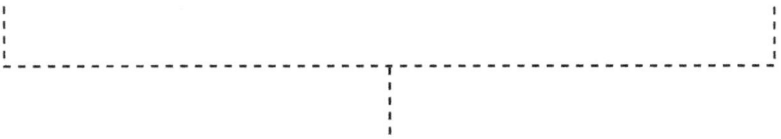

EVENT

**NOUN
+
VERB**

= Mount Everest Conquered

+ Mount Everest

+ Conquered

Each event is written on a post-it note, as a point in time, and will be stuck up on the sheets of paper as you build the plan. More event examples could be:

➡ **New ferry operating**

➡ **New bridge opened**

➡ **New product launched**

➡ **Book published**

An event is a point described by a noun + a verb.

▶ RELATIONSHIPS

PERT plans comprise EVENTS, linked by RELATIONSHIPS.

Before the ferry is operating, it has to be launched. Before it's launched, it has to be built.

Each event must be linked by at least two relationships to give the event a link to 'before' and 'after'. This is graphically shown in the diagrams.

▶ THE SEVEN STEPS OF GRAPHICAL PERT PLANNING

A graphical PERT plan is produced in seven simple steps.

Step 1 — Define major events

The first step is to review your vision and decide what key events must have occurred just before the vision becomes reality. These key events might be:

➡ **New sales force succeeding**

➡ **New computerised customer database operating**

➡ **Market share of 25% achieved**

➡ **Singapore office operating**

Each event is defined by a noun and a verb.

Each event is written on a post-it note.

Eventually you will end up with a graphical plan that looks something like the opposite diagram.

The first step is to establish the key events that occur just before the vision is finally a reality.

Agreeing on the key major events

The first part of Step 1 is to ask each person to write out (with one event per post-it note), all of the key events that have to have happened before the vision becomes a reality.

Then ask them to stick the post-it-notes up on a white board for sorting.

What happens is everybody has similar ideas on the key events.

The team groups and summarises all the post-its. Most visions are supported by between six to ten key events.

They generally summarise functional areas:

➡ New computer system working — **(systems)**

➡ New plant commissioned — **(manufacturing)**

➡ New advertising campaign succeeding — **(marketing)**

➡ Sales force training completed — **(sales)**

➡ New office facilities opened — **(admin)**

➡ New product launched — **(innovation)**

The first step, as the picture shows, is to establish your vision on the right-hand side of your field of view, with time flowing from left to right. Then decide the key events that underpin that vision, the major strategic areas.

Imagine each PERT planning chart is like a rope bridge across a river — with the events connected by the relationships. Your vision is on the far bank of the river. The river is raging and, as a metaphor, represents all the problems and challenges you will be presented with. Some people are happy just to jump into the river of life without planning and the river sweeps them away to mediocrity — or worse.

To secure the vision you and your team have co-created, you have to install planning rope bridges that link the near riverbank of 'now' — to the far river bank of the 'future' — where your vision exists.

You start on the far bank of the river in 'the future' and weave the PERT planning ropes back towards present time.

The key events underpinning the vision are like the pegs on the far bank of the river to which your PERT planning rope bridges will be attached.

Then work back in time, asking that same question — 'What happened just before that?', concentrating on the major events back across 'the river' of time.

Step 1 only focuses on the major events. There are usually about four or five major events. They form stepping stones back from the future vision to now, present time.

Clearly, there are many issues to be confronted, such as the demand for ferry services, including new technologies in ferry construction and conforming to possible new harbour regulations. However, these are handled in Step 2 when planning the detail.

At this stage we are only concerned with the major events. So if you were planning:

➡ **New Ferry Operating**

You would take a large step back in time by asking — 'What happened just before that?' — and you then might create another major event:

➡ **New Ferry Launched**

Clearly there is a great deal of commissioning and training work to be done between launching and operating a new ferry. But we are only initially concerned with the major events.

Then, taking another large step back asking the same question — 'What happened just before that?' — might lead you to a major event:

➡ **New Ferry Designed**

The question again — 'What happened just before that?

Another large step back -

➡ **Market Research Completed**

The question again — 'What happened just before that?'

➡ **New Ferry Route Planned**

The end result of the seven PERT planning steps will be to have your vision linked to this present time bank of the river by a set of detailed PERT planning rope bridges.

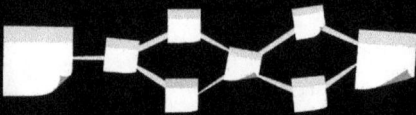

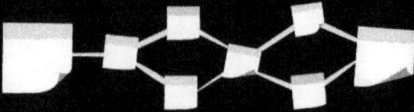

When all the rope planning bridges are in place, the whole team can see that the vision can be achieved.

They have to take action across each plan rope bridge by going forward towards the vision, one step at a time. Having planned back in time from the future, to avoid the three planning traps discussed, the plans are enacted forward from present time.

Step 2 — Define minor events

Taking the simple planning rope bridge outlined with four or five major events, the next step is to define the minor events. The same principles are involved. The minor events are still defined by a noun and a verb and you work backwards in time, inserting the minor events between the major events already established on the planning sheet of paper on the wall.

Start out in the future with the major event **'New Ferry Operating'** — followed by the question:

'What happened just before that?'

This defines the first minor event.

➡ **'All Equipment Commissioned'**

- followed by the question: 'What happened just before that?'

This defines the next minor event.

➡ **'Equipment Testing Completed'**

- followed by the question: 'What happened just before that?'

➡ **'Equipment Testing Commenced'**

This leads back in time to the next major event — **'New Ferry Launched.'**

You use the same principle in Step 2, asking the same question — 'What happened just before that?'

Just fill in the gaps with the minor events between the major events you defined in Step 1.

In a marketing example, you might have —

➡ **25% market share gained**

- preceded by

➡ **promotional campaign succeeds**

- preceded by

➡ **promotional campaign launched**

- preceded by

➡ **new product launched**

- preceded by

➡ **new product designed**

- preceded by

➡ **new product specified**

- preceded by

➡ **market research completed**

- preceded by

➡ **market research undertaken**

- preceded by

➡ **possible customer need identified.**

Step 3 — Sequence the events

You will find this is a powerful tool to choose the best course of action to achieve the vision. As you use the tool, you may find that your thinking patterns are very linear and sequential. You initially think about the events coming back in time in a single step by step process. That is OK.

Step 3 is to now sequence the events, because much of your plan can probably be carried out in parallel.

Planning the equipment testing could easily be done in parallel with training the new crew and developing a new timetable.

By using post-it's on the paper on the wall, you can move the events around and work to achieve as many parallel activities as possible.

This part of the seven step process takes time but it is the most rewarding. Remember at this stage you have introduced no relationships into the PERT rope bridge to link the events.

As you work with the events, gaps will become clear and, because the tool is so graphical and so flexible, you can easily write up more minor events (noun plus verb) on additional post-it notes and insert them where necessary.

Step 4 — Draw in relationships

Gradually the events, major and minor, which are part of the planning rope bridge, take shape. When the plan settles down, Step 4 is to draw in the relationships.

This is done by starting out in the future — on the right hand side of the plan — with the key event achieved and working back in time.

'What happened just before that?'

Then create the relationships between the events.

Working back from the future tests the logic flow of the plans you have developed.

Each event has to have at least two relationships — one joining it to the previous event — and one joining it to the next event.

There can be more than two relationships linking any one event as the diagram below shows.

As the relationships are established, the reason for taking your time on Step 3 of sequencing the events, before moving to Step 4 of establishing relationships, becomes clear.

Because, as you work on establishing the relationships, working back from the future, sequencing distinctions are made and events continue to move around on the paper.

Take your time on Step 3. Do not be in a rush to get to Step 4.

Eventually, the relationships stabilise and, as the plan develops, you see why the metaphor of a rope bridge is perfect for graphical PERT planning.

Step 5 — Allocate resources

Once the graphical planning rope bridge is in place, with both events and relationships, Step 5 is to allocate resources.

As events are 'achieved' points in time, the resources are allocated to the relationships.

People, time and money are the main resources. A relationship can require people, time and money to complete.

This one might take three people, two weeks and a budget of $10,000 between the two events.

Step 6 — Calculate resources required

Once the resources are allocated, Step 6 is to calculate the total resources required across the planning rope bridge — the number of people, the total cost and the total time it will take.

Step 7 — Establish deadlines

The seventh step is to establish deadlines.

There may be deadlines by which something has to be achieved. The sales targets 'event' may have to be achieved by a specific date.

The new ferry operating 'event' must be achieved by a specific date.

There may be points on the PERT rope bridge before which an activity cannot commence. Perhaps a software update is required and will not be available until next April — so you can't start work till then.

If your goal is to climb Mount Everest, you can't start till the monsoon season finishes in October. You must be off the mountain before the monsoon starts the following May.

So deadlines and start times need to be defined — both in terms of the resources needed to cross the PERT rope bridge — and what has to be done by whom, by when — if the planning rope bridge is to be successfully crossed.

Review the plan

The power of graphical PERT plans is that the whole team is involved, working on separate planning rope bridges. At the end of the planning exercise, the whole team can review the vision, the key events and the PERT planning rope bridge attached to each key event.

▶ ACTIVATING THE PLANS

Once the planning rope bridges are in place, you can then activate the plan from current time into the future.

STEP 1 – DEFINE MAJOR EVENTS

New Ferry route planned

Market Research completed

New Ferry designed

New Ferry launched

New Ferry operating

'What happened just before that?'

STEP 2 – DEFINE MINOR EVENTS

New Ferry launched

Equipment Testing Commenced

Equipment Testing Completed

All equipment Commissioned

New Ferry operating

STEP 3 – SEQUENCE THE EVENTS

New Ferry Launched

Equipment Testing Commissioned

All Testing Completed

All Equipment Commissioned

New Timetable Developed

New Timetable Published

New Ferry Operating

New Crew Hired

Training Commenced

Training Completed

STEP 4 – DRAW IN RELATIONSHIPS

New Ferry Launched

Equipment Testing Commissioned

All Testing Completed

All Equipment Commissioned

New Timetable Developed

New Timetable Published

New Ferry Operating

New Crew Hired

Training Commenced

Training Completed

STEP 5 – ALLOCATE RESOURCES

STEP 6 – CALCULATE RESOURCES REQUIRED

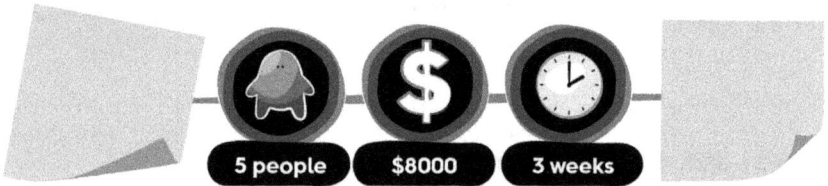

5 people $8000   3 weeks

STEP 7 – ESTABLISH DEADLINES

REVIEW THE PLAN

PERT

The power of both the vision and the graphical PERT plan combined, is that your team can see the vision and the concrete plans that, once enacted, will make the vision a reality.

The PERT planning tool, combined with the vision, provide a daily sense of direction. When the 'builders' (your team) show up, they can see what they are creating and what needs to be done each day.

You will find this a very powerful tool. Many others have. Enthusiasm and motivation are inspired when a way forward towards the vision is clear to all.

The Planning Room

If you can, it is best to set up a Planning Room. A Planning Room is a meeting room dedicated to — you guessed it — planning.

Why create a Planning Room?

The reason is this. A large vision attracts large resistance, you will need to be well organised with strong response strategies to combat them and succeed.

As time goes by, critical data emerges and joins the growing visual data base on the walls of the Planning Room.

Discussion and decision quality improves as your team can visually access a vast array of pertinent data.

PERT is a powerful graphical tool. The whole team can clearly see the deadlines to be met, when various actions commence and how different team activities are linked to a common destiny — the vision achieved.

If you have a major vision, and set of plans which will take months or perhaps even years to achieve, you may choose to take the graphical plans and put them into a planning software package. Using a software planning product forces the discipline of allocating resources.

The Spirit Being within each team member realises that this game called 'let's achieve the vision' can be won — and it might even be a lot of fun!

▶ TEAM DECISION MAKING

The great advantage of a Planning Room — displaying both your vision and the graphical PERT plans — is that you have created a visual framework for high calibre team decision making.

When a problem shows up, options can be reviewed and decisions made using the vision and graphical PERT plans as reference guides.

▶ SUMMARY

You now have a vision that is 'out there' in the future, inspiring your team forward.

It is now linked to the present by a set of graphical PERT plans giving you and your team clear plans of action.

Progress can be visually ticked off as time passes. You already have the passion keys to motivate and inspire enthusiasm.

In the next chapter, we will explore how understanding the power of the mind can improve the quality of your planning.

We will also explore the nature of reality creation and how graphical vision, and graphical PERT planning combined, fire up each team member so they are at full power — the 16-cylinder engine.

These tools are your secret weapon for achieving consistently outstanding results. I've seen them work time and time again across hundreds of organisations around the world. Why not give them a go?

FOURTEEN

THE POWER OF THE MIND

Your goal is to achieve a vision with your team by enacting clear plans of action.

This chapter shows you how to use the power of the mind for an additional edge.

It also demonstrates why graphical vision and graphical planning tools are vital for achieving success.

▶ THREE TOOLS OF PLANNING

The 16-cylinder BMES model — body, mind, emotions and spirit — has three cylinders that are physical (the body) and 13-cylinders that are metaphysical (mind, emotions and spirit).

Here lies the clue to higher leverage planning.

There are three tools you have at your disposal in developing your clear plans of action to achieve the vision.

Two involve the physics and the third involves metaphysics — and is much more powerful.

Tool 1 — Your body

The first planning tool is your body.

You can develop a clear plan of action, then run around 24 hours a day enacting that plan.

Just using your body to do all the work is the way to an early grave. It is low leverage not to mention tiring.

Tool 2 — Your team

You can obtain more leverage by enlisting the help of a team.

You could then encourage more 'busyness' by having your whole team run around 24 hours a day getting the job done!

Only three of the 16 BMES (body, mind, emotions and spirit) cylinders are physical. So, you and your team running around 24 hours a day enacting your plans is also a low leverage activity.

Tool 3 — Your Mind, Emotions and Spirit

High leverage planning and action must involve the 13-cylinders of the metaphysics — the mind, emotions and spirit.

An understanding of metaphysics is far from commonplace in business. Western school and business education encompasses no area of metaphysics.

The power of the mind is, however, starting to be recognised as this quote demonstrates:

'Leaders of the future are likely to be more dependent on intuitive sensitivity.'
ALVIN TOFFLER, POWER SHIFT

We will now explore a set of simple metaphysical planning tools that will enhance your life journey skills and help you achieve your vision.

▶ KEYS TO THE MIND

The mind is a powerful bio-computer. Everyone on your team possesses one.

Unfortunately, most of us are never taught how to access its full power.

This chapter helps you and your team access the power of the mind to improve your ability to succeed.

A detailed guide on how to harness the full powers of the mind has been laid out in the famous book Think and Grow Rich.

Napoleon Hill interviewed 504 of the world's most successful people, iconic names such as Henry Ford, Thomas Edison, the Wright brothers, Rockefeller, Woolworth and Gillette.

It may surprise you that the keys to their success was not in physical planning — but rather in metaphysical planning.

Think and Grow Rich is really a manual to explain the power of metaphysics — the mind, emotions and the spirit.

Those interviewed by Napoleon Hill were true business pioneers who knew how to tap into their inner strength.

The metaphysical planning approach is nicely summarised by the inventor and genius, Nikola Tesla:

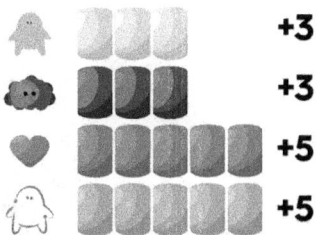

+3

+3

+5

+5

= 16

'My method is different. I do not rush into actual work. When I get a new idea, I start at once building it up in my imagination, and make improvements and operate the device in my mind...'

NIKOLA TESLA

You see the 'bias for action' trap as senior management work longer and longer hours, going from meeting to meeting, using their journeymen experience to battle the ever present sense of urgency and crisis, never optimising the metaphysical leverage of themselves or their people.

Buckminster Fuller explained that the leadership leverage challenge is a generalised principle he called ephemeralisation — doing more and more with less and less.

In the physical world, you see this generalised principle of ephemeralisation everywhere. The change from valves to transistors to silicon chips is a classic example of doing more with less, as is the communication evolution from smoke signals and drums to letters to Morse code telegraph to fax to Internet and e-mail. We have improved telecommunications from using chunky copper cables to hair-like strands of glass fibre, doing more and more with less and less. Using more mind energy in thinking and planning — rather than using the physical energy of action and doing — is a major ephemeralisation step.

This is a critical skill in choosing a more efficient approach.

Let's now explore how to use the bio-computer of the mind.

▶ A BIO-COMPUTER USER'S MANUAL

Think and Grow Rich provides operating rules for working with the highest leverage planning tool of all — the human mind.

We will explore planning, creativity and original thought using the bio-computer of the mind to ensure you get the results you want and, in business, move way ahead of your competition to achieve your success vision.

There are tools available that will enable you to harness the extraordinary bio-computing power of the mind that every organisation is paying for but very few are using.

You will see that the metaphysical tools for success are already in your possession.

Let's review some of the quotes from Think & Grow Rich to see how you can use the wisdom and knowledge they contain to achieve your success vision. Success leaves footprints.

▶ THOUGHTS ARE THINGS

Thoughts are things.

Thoughts — in the realm of the metaphysics of the mind — are just as real as physical objects.

Your vision and PERT plan are powerful thoughts amplified through pictures.

The human mind is very visual and the full power of graphical vision and graphical PERT planning will become apparent as we move through this chapter.

▶ WE MOVE TOWARDS OUR DOMINANT THOUGHTS

We move towards our dominant thoughts.

As thoughts are metaphysical things, if you program your thoughts (your vision and PERT milestone events) into the human bio-computer, the mind becomes a goal-seeking device.

Significant vision has significant metaphysical mass and activates the law of metaphysical gravity — attracting the people and resources you need for success.

You too are drawn forward by that same metaphysical gravity pulling you towards the vision and goals you have created. You move towards your dominant thoughts — your vision and goals.

This chapter shows you how to access and program the deeper parts of your mind to harness metaphysical gravity.

Enhancing life journey skills requires us to take responsibility for our circumstances and our life journey and accept that we do create our own reality from what we think about.

In the realm of thought, your graphical vision and PERT plan events are your goals — statements of what you want to achieve. These goal thoughts can be energised by the passion and desire of your emotions and the enthusiasm and commitment of your spirit.

Programming these vision and PERT event goal thoughts into the deeper parts of the mind is like broadcasting them into an intelligent metaphysical universe.

The intelligent universe then responds like a giant feedback machine giving you indications of progress and encouragement if you are on the right track (we call these ticks) and little taps on the shoulder if you are 'off track', allowing you to take corrective action towards your vision.

The power of these mind tools means you do not have to have all the answers to start with.

Often, the universal intelligence feedback system comes up with unexpected alternative solutions on the journey towards the vision. We'll cover this later in this chapter when reviewing the power of the mastermind.

To optimise contact and alignment with your own reality creating mechanism, you need to understand how to use the deeper parts of your mind to broadcast the strongest possible signal of what you want.

A common problem for individuals, families and organisations with a weak vision — or no vision — is that they are so vulnerable to others' visions, goals and thoughts. Just as an asteroid is drawn to the larger physical mass of the sun rather than the Earth, strong visions, goals and thoughts exert more pulling power than weak ones.

Whatever your vision and goals are for your life, there will always be other people and groups with their counter visions and goals of what they want for and from you. These counter visions and goals of others may act at right angles or be diametrically opposed to your own aspirations.

As an example, it seems the banks' mortgage vision for you may not align with your personal and family vision of financial independence, security and freedom!

The word mortgage derives from the old French words 'mors' and 'gage' — pledged till death.

To counter-act the 'noise' from others, you need to broadcast the strongest possible vision and signals for what you want.

Otherwise you may not be influential enough to achieve your vision of success. That is why, in earlier chapters, we first covered the tools to develop strong graphical vision anchored with comprehensive graphical PERT plans.

This chapter shows you how to access the deepest parts of your mind to send out the strongest vision and goal 'signals'.

Imagine the signal strength of your business if everyone on your team used these powerful mind tools.

Let's start by looking at the structure of the bio-computer of the mind. This will provide you with the keys to program your mind, and the minds of your team, for maximum power.

▶ THE STRUCTURE OF OUR BIO-COMPUTER — THE MIND

There are three parts to the bio-computer of the mind, the conscious mind, the subconscious mind and the superconscious mind.

The conscious mind

The conscious mind is the part of your mind you know.

If you have never observed your conscious mind, just pause here. Close your eyes for a couple of minutes and just observe.

What was happening in your mind? Was it spinning along, only partially under your control, with many thoughts just appearing? Was it blank?

If your conscious mind is like mine, it goes at a speedy pace! Some thoughts you control, some just seem to appear and disappear.

If you pay attention for long enough, you may conclude that you are not totally in control of the thoughts that stream into your conscious mind.

Your bio-computer seems to generate output (thoughts) from programs you are unaware of. Some outputs probably seem disjointed, almost random.

The subconscious mind

Beneath the surface of the conscious mind lies the subconscious mind — which psychiatrists such as Sigmund Freud spent their lives exploring.

The subconscious mind is below our conscious awareness. It is a powerful part of the mind that runs multiple programs that keep you functioning.

Mind

Conscious

Subconscious

Superconscious

Mind

Conscious
Laptop

Subconscious
Mainframe

Superconcious
Supercomputer

If you wonder at the complexity of your digestive system or your self-healing abilities, you will realise the power of your subconscious bio-computer.

If it's clever enough to figure all that out, do you think it could help you to achieve your team's plans and vision?

The superconscious mind

Deeper still in our minds lies the realm of the superconscious, which fascinated psychiatrists such as Carl Jung in his exploration of the collective unconscious.

The superconscious is very esoteric terrain for most of us. Imagine accessing wisdom and intuition from universal intelligence to improve your plans and realise your vision. Now that is real bio-computing power and planning leverage.

Maximum bio-computer leverage

To leverage the full power of your bio-computer, you need to understand how to access the conscious mind, the subconscious mind and the superconscious mind.

If we are to use a computer analogy, the conscious mind is a personal computer or laptop. It has a reasonable processing power, but is limited nonetheless.

Researchers have shown that most of us can hold about five things in our conscious mind at any one time. It is not a powerful computer compared with the subconscious mind.

Continuing the analogy, the subconscious mind can be viewed as a mainframe and the superconscious is like a supercomputer.

If you want to have excellent plans that harness all of the available intelligence of you and your team, where would you run the programs to analyse your planning options? In the relatively small work station of the conscious mind or would you put the challenge of achieving your vision into the mainframe or the supercomputer?

If your vision is the stretch that it should be — something significant yet to do — then you need maximum bio-computer processing power. You need to know how to access the super bio-computers of you and your team.

Large geological survey analysis computer programs can take hours if not days to run, even on a supercomputer. You need this sort of processing power too.

The power of your superconscious dwarfs the processing power of the conscious mind.

Think and Grow Rich is about how to program the awesome power of the superconscious, your super bio-computer.

How do you think people like the Wright brothers, Henry Ford and Andrew Carnegie achieved such success? Were they really so much smarter than the rest of us? Or were they accessing an advantage not known to most?

Henry Ford left school in 1879 at 16 to become a machinist apprentice in Detroit, he didn't have the privilege of a full education. He had to figure things out for himself.

Andrew Carnegie had no formal education. He went to the US from Scotland in 1848 at 13 and started work in a cotton mill. He never went to school.

The business masters interviewed in Think and Grow Rich discovered the principles of metaphysical success from experience.

Let us now have a detailed look at their instructions and comment on each so you can maximise the use of your mind and those on your team to achieve your vision.

▶ REVIEWING THE QUOTES FROM THINK AND GROW RICH

Thoughts are Things

'We move towards Dominant Thoughts.'

If you setup your graphical vision and PERT events as clear thought goals, they have a metaphysical reality. They exert metaphysical gravitational attraction and your bio-computer works out ways to achieve these goals — to bring them from the metaphysics of thought into the physical reality of results.

Desire

'There are no limitations to the mind except those we acknowledge.'

This sentence is so simple and yet so powerful. You and your team have access to unlimited bio-computer processing power. You just need to learn how to harness it.

Faith

'All thoughts which have been emotionalised (given feeling) and mixed with faith begin immediately to translate themselves into their physical equivalent or counterpart.'

This sentence is also almost unbelievable in its statement — that our metaphysical thoughts create our physical reality.

Thought (three cylinders of mind) plus emotion (five cylinders of emotion) plus faith (faith is in the spirit domain so five cylinders) means harnessing the 13-cylinders of metaphysics.

'Faith is to believe what we do not see, and the reward of this faith is to see what we believe.'
SAINT AUGUSTINE

The power to realise your vision lies in the metaphysics of you and your team.

Auto-suggestion

'For amazing results, get the deepest part of your mind to go to work for you. Back this with emotion power and the combination is terrific.'

Specialised Knowledge

'You find the knowledge that takes you where you want to go.'

This is just common sense.

Imagination

'Imagination is the workshop of your mind, capable of turning mind energy into accomplishment and wealth.'

Transforming the metaphysical mind energy of planning into physical accomplishment and results.

Organised Planning

'It is necessary to plan and to organise in order to get rich. Staying poor is easy, poverty needs no plan.'

No comment required!

Decision

'Lack of decision is a major cause of failure. A made-up mind attunes itself to tremendous extra power.'

Persistence

'Persistence is an essential factor in the procedure. The basis of persistence is the power of will.'

The will is located in the solar plexus. You must learn to contact and use your will power. It is a vital leadership skill. Will power is demonstrated by the power of intent.

The word intent is derived from the Latin 'in tendere' — to stretch towards — your vision.

Power of the Mastermind

'Great power can be accumulated through no other principle.'

We will cover this mastermind principle in depth in this chapter.

The Subconscious Mind

'Your subconscious mind waits like a sleeping giant to back up every plan and purpose.'

If the subconscious (bio-computer) is sleeping, it won't process your vision plans. This chapter shows you how to wake it up and use it.

The Brain

'You find amazing new powers in every part of your mind.'

Most people simply don't know how to use their bio-computer. The power that's unlocked when you do will amaze you.

The Sixth Sense

'Inspirations and hunches no longer pass you by.'

This is when the laws of metaphysics start to work for you and your team because you are using them consciously.

You can now start to see the scope of Think and Grow Rich and the empowering messages and tools that Andrew Carnegie wanted to share with us.

▶ PROGRAMMING THE SUPER BIO-COMPUTER

Now you understand that everyone on your team has a super bio-computer.

The next question is — how do you access and program it?

It is very simple. Programming the supercomputer is done initially by goal setting and creating the vision.

There are several key rules that are essential for goals to be used correctly in programming the mind.

▶ BIO COMPUTER PROGRAMMING — GOAL SETTING

Goals are events you wish to occur.

The important key to goal setting is to be clear on the goal. Don't worry too much about how to achieve it — that is the job of your super bio-computer, to figure out the 'how.'

Your vision achieved is a goal. Any event on the graphical PERT planning rope bridges can be a goal.

Goal setting rule 1 — facts and feelings

The first rule of goal setting is that the goals must involve facts and feeling.

It is April 15th, and the team is feeling super excited to take delivery of our new mark 4 research spectroscope.

Why is it important that the goal involves facts and feeling?

Because research shows that our brain functions in two halves — the left brain and the right brain.

The left brain is the domain of facts, logic, numbers, data and quantitative analysis.

The right brain is intuitive and involves emotions, qualitative information, and pictures.

Including both data and emotions in the goal means it can be worked on by both the left and the right sides of the brain.

Why not use the bio-computing power available to you?

Goal setting rule 2 — present tense

The second rule of goal setting is that goals must be written in the present tense. The reason? Time is a construct of the conscious mind.

In the subconscious and the superconscious mind, time does not exist — there is only the eternal 'now'.

A goal, once inserted into the bio-computer, can be processed only in the subconscious and superconscious if it is written in the present tense.

If you write the goal in the future tense, 'I will be living in my new home by the end of next year', the super bio-computer scans the future tense 'will' — and nothing happens.

If you write your goals in the past tense, 'I have bought my new home, I did it', the super bio-computer scans the past tense 'have' — and again does nothing.

It is October 20th; our new radio astronomy dish is being commissioned and made ready for use.

Many people find it challenging to write goals in the present tense. You know that the goal is not yet achieved, it is a future event.

Just be mindful that the future tense 'will be' or the past tense 'have' do not creep into your bio-computer goal setting programming.

Goal setting rule 3 — visualise the goal achieved

The third rule of goal setting is that you regularly close your eyes and visualise the goal.

Visualising pictures is required because the right brain thinks in pictures.

If you and your team have done the work creating the vision and graphical PERT plans — this should be easy.

Goal setting rule 4 — goals must be yours

Goals must be yours — and you must want them.

No one's bio-computer will be fired up by goals imposed by someone else. The emotions, the commitment and the enthusiasm of the spirit must be real.

The power of your emotions and spirit are keys to your bio-computer power.

Goal setting rule 5 — short-term and long-term goals must be logically consistent

For the bio-computer to compile your goal programs they must be logically consistent.

My long-term goal is achieving financial independence over the next five years and my short-term goal is spending more time with my family than ever before.

This sounds highly unlikely as a logical strategy and may not run successfully as a bio-computer program.

Goal setting rule 6 — goals must follow your values

Your goals must align with your values.

My long-term goal is being financially free and working for Greenpeace voluntarily. To achieve this, I am salesman of the year selling large numbers of anti-personnel land mines for my company.

These are inconsistent goals and will not run on the bio-computer because they are contradictory in terms of spirit integrity.

▶ BIO-COMPUTER PROGRAMMING INSERTING THE PROGRAMS

It is not enough just to set the goals. You have to learn how to install them into the super bio-computer.

It is possible just to read or affirm the goals repeatedly to insert them into the PC of the conscious mind.

There is, however, a much more powerful technique you can use to program the super bio-computer. It will work on your goals and also give you additional ideas on how to achieve your plan and vision.

The technique is very simple.

The technique imprints your goals on to the surface of the subconscious mind. First, you need to understand a little more of the way the mind functions.

You may have seen biofeedback machines where researchers hook up electrodes to the surface of the skull and read the frequency of the brainwaves being generated.

Beta waves

Normal conscious thinking shows up as relatively high frequency brain waves, between 13 and 25 cycles per second. Researchers call these Beta patterns.

If you close your eyes and observe your conscious mind, you will relate to the conscious mind being a high frequency, speedy place most of the time.

Alpha waves

Below the level of conscious thinking is the realm of dreaming, the domain of alpha waves. These have a frequency bandwidth of between eight to thirteen cycles per second. This is the threshold of the subconscious.

Theta waves

In deep sleep, our brain emits theta waves. These are slower, longer frequencies in the range four to eight cycles per second.

Research shows we go down into deep sleep and enter a dreaming state several times a night. So, we go down into Theta, up into Alpha, down into Theta.

Our brain patterns change. While we are in Alpha we dream — and we dream in pictures.

You can see the eyes of a sleeping person move under their eyelids as they literally watch the dream pictures in their mind. Researchers call it REM — rapid eye movements.

Delta waves

Below the realm of Theta waves are Delta brain waves at four cycles per second. This is unconsciousness.

Inserting the goal program

The goal program insertion technique is a process whereby you slow down your brainwaves, from their normal speedy Beta to the calmer slower Alpha state — and this is the doorway to the subconscious and the superconscious.

The way to do this is to close your eyes and in sequence, imagine the colours of the rainbow:

➡ **Red Orange Yellow Green Blue Purple Violet**

Waves

β	Beta	
α	Alpha	
θ	Theta	
Δ	Delta	

Red

Orange

Yellow

Green

Blue

Purple

Violet

The colours slow the brain waves because each colour affects our mood — and therefore our mental state.

Religions and royalty have known of the power of colour for millenia. High church ministers wear purple robes, Buddhist monks wear saffron robes.

Research has confirmed this knowledge by measuring our brain waves using biofeedback.

First, imagine yourself surrounded by the colour red. The colour red induces a certain level of physical relaxation in the body so stay with it for a couple of minutes.

Then visualise yourself immersed in the colour orange, then yellow, then green and on through the colours of the rainbow — blue to purple to violet. Stay with each colour for about a minute.

As you observe each colour in sequence, your mind will slow down.

After imagining violet, let your imagination drift to a peaceful scene, a scene of your choice. Some people choose a favourite countryside spot, a deserted beach, sitting on a cloud. It doesn't matter. It's your mind, your peaceful scene.

This is a great tool for general relaxation and a mind programming tool. If you have a sleep deficit — and most of us do — you may initially drift off to sleep. There is nothing wrong with that. However, with a little practice, you can comfortably imagine a peaceful scene.

You are now accessing your imagination.

You will build and utilise an imagination workshop of the mind.

The next step of this goal and vision program insertion process is to clear a space in your peaceful scene and build a stage and a cinema screen, much like the old drive-in movie screens.

You can build your stage and cinema screen with whatever materials you want to.

It is your mind and your imagination workshop.

So, in your mind, build a stage and stairs leading up on to it, with a big cinema screen at the back of the stage.

On the right hand side of the screen build a green door and on the left hand side, a blue door.

Goal projection

In your imagination, project your goal or vision, the result you want, on to the cinema screen as though you are running a movie.

As you play your 'goal movie', feel the emotions of success.

Include a date somewhere in your movie so that the subconscious has a date to work with.

See the customers signing the contract.

See your team mates overjoyed at such huge success.

See yourself and your family moving into the beautiful new house.

This is the way to insert your goal programs into the subconscious bio-computer.

The second part of the process is that, instead of a flat cinema screen, imagine you are at the entrance to a huge hologram — a three dimensional image you can actually walk into.

Imagine being there — and how you feel — when your success is achieved. It is happening all around you. Feel it. Sense it.

See the calendar with your own eyes. Taste the champagne at the victory celebration.

Listen to your colleagues talking excitedly at the success of the vision achieved.

In this second exercise, the goal is re-emphasised onto the surface of the subconscious.

Remember thoughts are things and we move towards our dominant thoughts.

By inserting the program of the desired goal into the subconscious, you are programming the powerful parts of your mind to move towards the new dominant thought — your vision being achieved.

The metaphysical gravity pull of envisaged success is activated.

Always use the present tense — the here and now.

Even though the calendar says a future date, you are behaving as though you are there now.

You can sequentially run several goals.

Simply step back out of the holographic image, back on to the stage and allowing the screen to become blank again between goal projections.

In this way you can activate the deeper and more powerful parts of your mind to help you achieve several goals and get the results you need — this is Life Journey Skills in action.

▶ PROGRAM OUTPUT

The powerful subconscious and superconscious will provide solutions. Some solutions will arrive as good ideas, some as intuitions.

Sometimes somebody will say something to you. They may not realise the power of what they just said, but you will. The Universal Intelligence feedback machine has multiple communication channels.

▶ THE MASTERMIND

It is important to mention the section of Think and Grow Rich that covers the power of the mastermind, because the green door in your workshop of the mind has special significance for using the principle of the mastermind.

'Great power can be accumulated through no other principle.'

The mastermind principle has two applications — physical and psychic.

Napoleon Hill explained that the physical mastermind is a relatively simple concept to understand, whereas the psychic mastermind can be more challenging — given that most people's understanding of metaphysics is limited.

First let's explore the physical mastermind and second, the psychic mastermind, to guide your success.

The physical mastermind

The physical principle of the mastermind is simple.

The physical mastermind is described as two or more people gathered together regularly, as a team, putting their minds on to solving or achieving the common challenge. Their journeyman experience is focused and you can achieve more with a set of focused minds than you can on your own. This makes sense.

Different people = different perspectives, different experiences, different ideas.

Who is on your physical mastermind? Who are you bringing together, regularly, to discuss the plan and the vision?

As you go forward, the aliens of resistance are bound to show up. So even the best visions and PERT plans need regular mastermind meetings to discuss progress and obstacles.

Perhaps your physical mastermind is your team — and that's fine. Just remember that the key to a successful mastermind is that it has to meet regularly. So how regularly does your whole team meet?

Do you ensure quality time for your planning? Or do you have people interrupting, taking messages and phone calls? What sort of physical mastermind are you regularly running?

As our children were growing up, my wife and I held regular, clearly identified family mastermind meetings with our boys to discuss everyone's goals and plans. We sometimes went out to lunch as a family to make it a special occasion for them and us.

Harnessing the power of other minds, in a well-chosen physical mastermind, is imperative for your success.

Don't surround yourself with 'yes people'. Surround yourself with people who ask more of you than you do, people who will be straight with you and face the truth, people playing win/win, people with courage — 16-cylinder people.

Check your current physical mastermind members for these qualities.

Are there people who should be removed or anyone who should be added?

This is not about position or status, it's about the qualities they bring to the mastermind to help you.

If you don't have a current physical mastermind, take the time to draw up your ideal list of people, then approach them, explain the principle, and ask them to join you. What have you got to lose?

Top Tip: You must be very careful of who you surround yourself with. It can make or break your chances of success.

The psychic mastermind

The psychic principle of the mastermind is explained in Think and Grow Rich:

'The psychic phase of the mastermind principle is much more difficult to comprehend. You may catch a significant suggestion from this statement.

No two minds ever come together without thereby creating a third invisible, intangible force which may be likened to third mind.'

Just read that sentence again. 'No two minds ever come together without thereby creating a third, invisible, intangible force which may be likened to a third mind.'

The Bible says:

'Where two or three are gathered together in my name, there am I in the midst of them.'
MATTHEW 18:20

When you focus on a challenge with more than one mind, additional mind power kicks in, 'Where two or three are gathered together in my name, there am I in the midst of them.'

It doesn't say — 'If you show up, I'll show up.' That is why you need to have a mastermind group to help you achieve your vision.

The Christian Bible has interesting insights on how to use the bio-computer power of the mind. Eastern religions also understand this power. The same concepts are reflected in the Koran and the Hadith sayings of the Prophet Mohammed.

'But when you pray, go into a room by yourself, shut the door, and pray to your Father who is there in the secret place, and your Father who sees what is secret will reward you.' Read Matthew 6:6

I am not a theologian, but I think that 'the secret place' is the workshop of the mind, the doorway to the subconscious and the superconscious.

Note the verb — 'and your father who sees' — it is visual.

Even though we usually 'say' our prayers — audio, the bio-computer works better with visuals.

▶ FAITH

FAITH can be an acronym — Father and I Together Here.

As you work with the awesome potential of your bio-computer and the untapped bio-computers on your team, have faith that a higher power exists and you can consciously call on it.

- ➡ **Christians call this higher power Father and speak of divine intervention.**
- ➡ **North American Indians call it Great Spirit.**
- ➡ **Hindu people call it Brahma.**
- ➡ **People of Islamic faith call it Allah.**
- ➡ **Others call it Universal Intelligence or Source.**

We are working with the super-conscious.

The power of the psychic mastermind works best if you ensure you have an empty chair at your planning meetings.

I would not dream of running a corporate workshop — or a public presentation — without two chairs up on the stage with me.

Why two? If I sit down on one during the workshop, there is always an empty chair for the third mind to join the minds of myself and the audience.

'Where two or three are gathered together' — the psychic mastermind shows up. The chair is a visual metaphor, a reminder of that.

Is the concept of a psychic mastermind creating cognitive dissonance for you?

Possibly. But if it worked so well for earlier generations of highly successful people, maybe it can help you and your team.

The physical and psychic mastermind concepts are powerful. You would do well to consider using them if you wish achieve success in your life — whatever success means to you and the people around you.

'Imagination is more important than knowledge. For knowledge is limited, whereas imagination embraces the

entire world, stimulating progress, giving birth to evolution.'

ALBERT EINSTEIN

▶ THE IMAGINARY MASTERMIND

You can use the power of the psychic mastermind in the imaginary workshop of your mind.

Once you've projected your goals onto the screen of your workshop, you are now ready to use the power of the green door.

Behind the green door is the person you would like to bring onto your psychic mastermind — a wise being with whom you can mentally discuss your goals and plans. Using the psychic mastermind principle works best at this deep level — the doorway to the super bio- computer.

Clearly the wise being is an iconic representation of your own superconscious. Napoleon Hill reports bringing in a whole boardroom of advisers. It really doesn't matter — it is up to you, have fun with it!

This is an amazing tool for accessing your superconscious.

Read Matthew 7:7-8 as a mind manual:

'Ask, and it shall be given you. Seek, and ye shall find, knock, and it shall be opened unto you. For everyone that asketh receiveth, and he that seeketh findeth, and to him that knocketh it shall be opened.'

How did Einstein develop his theories of relativity?

Not by just using his conscious mind.

He was lying on his back in a field, in the sunshine, looking up at the blue sky and daydreaming. He wondered what it would like to be a sunbeam radiating out from the sun into space. As he did this, he found himself as an imaginary sunbeam on a curved trajectory.

What a jolt this was to his left-brain, logical, conscious mind.

The rest — quantum theory and relativity — as they say, is history.

Explore the technique. Decide who you want to invite in to give you wise counsel.

In your imagination workshop, view your goals on the screen and experience them actually happening around you. Then let the screen fade blank. Then imagine walking across the stage to the green door.

Open the door and invite your psychic mastermind guest in.

In your imagination, invite the person in, thank them for coming, explain your goals and then ask them if they have any advice or guidance. Then listen. You may be amazed at the calibre and quality of the advice you receive.

It may be completely outside the normal logic sequences of what you would expect. Alternative ideas and strategies may be presented.

When you have finished explaining each goal and asking for feedback, ask your wise mastermind being if there is anything else you should know at this point.

Again, listen.

Then, thank them for coming, ask them if it is okay for you to invite them again.

The Blue Door Recharge

Now once again, you are alone on the stage of your imaginary workshop. The final step is to imagine walking across the stage to the other side of the screen to the blue door.

Open the blue door, step over the threshold and drift into the colour blue. You will find that the colour blue is deeply and powerfully relaxing — a great way to refresh your spirit.

Once you have drifted through the colour blue for up to 20 minutes, in your own time and at your own speed, come back to full conscious alertness. Surround yourself with the rainbow colours in the reverse order, from blue to red. In your own time, wiggle your toes, stretch your fingers and open your eyes.

The colour blue has deep significance and power. We say to each other, where did that idea come from? I don't know, it just came out of the...? The blue!

The word idea derives from the Latin 'id deo' — that from god.

▶ YOUR ACTIONS NOW?

So, now that you know how to plan your life journey using the power of the mind — how will you put this into action?

You could remain low leverage by using the vision you have co-created and the PERT rope bridge plans you have developed.

You may be satisfied to hire high calibre people and let them run using just their own conscious minds. However, why not access the power of their super bio-computers, and the psychic power of the master mind, and go for gold medal results?

▶ THE MIND-PLANNING TOOL IN ACTION

Case Study

The senior marketing team of a large client's organisation was intrigued by our discussions about high leverage planning using the power of the mind. So we ran a psychic mastermind session to elicit the key competitive differentials for their organisation into the future.

We used the technique of going down through the colours of the rainbow, setting up the stage and screen in the imagination workshop of the mind, visualising the goals and then inviting in the psychic mastermind.

Before we initiated the activity, we agreed on a set of questions they wanted to ask their collective psychic masterminds. What were the advantages available to their organisation, how should they use them, were there any pitfalls, what were the biggest problem areas and how should they overcome them?

When the marketing team had agreed to the set of questions — and each individual had decided who they would invite into their workshop of the mind as their personal psychic mastermind — we started the exercise.

Everyone closed their eyes and I guided the team down through the colours. They created their own individual peaceful scenes and imaginary workshops. They ran their goals and visions individually on their 'mind screens' and entered the 3D holograms of success achieved.

Then each person welcomed his or her psychic mastermind visitor.

I slowly read the questions aloud one by one. They asked their psychic mastermind guest the question and made notes of the answers received on a pad in front, with their eyes closed.

After the session, each person had a few minutes of private dialogue with his or her mastermind icon asking for personal guidance. They then asked the mastermind icon to leave and after some minutes behind the blue door drifting in deep relaxation, the group came back up through the colours.

They then broke into small groups of two or three to discuss the experience. It was not your average corporate strategic planning meeting of the 20th century, but it might well be in the 21st and 22nd centuries.

The team were amazed.

First, several had been visited by the same icon (an old Tibetan monk).

Second, in the group of 14 people, the answers they received independently, were very similar.

Even though the company is a high technology company, the answers were that the sustainable differential advantage did not lie with their advanced use of technology; it lay with their people, their culture and their level of customer service.

There were many more distinctions.

The Managing Director of their advertising agency was present at the session and the agency went on to make a very powerful TV advertisement that incorporated the themes from that session including the Tibetan monk. The ad generated huge response and the company continued to grow.

I have facilitated similar planning sessions to explore areas really challenging for the logical mind.

Are there specific mineral deposits in a certain rock structure?

What is the best way of tackling customer service?

How do we best market accounting services in the 21st century?

Using the tool takes courage. The technique is not infallible.

It is however a powerful tool you can add to your tool kit — Vision Creation, PERT planning, and using the Super Bio-Computer.

Why not try it? What have you got to lose?

▶ BIO-COMPUTER TIME STORAGE

To ensure you have the best planning capability possible, there is one more tool we should review while covering the power of the mind to optimise your life. This tool evaluates how people store time in their own bio-computer.

This tool is easier to use if you have a partner.

One person closes their eyes. Their partner then asks them to physically point to 'Now' with their outstretched finger in the space around them.

They identify — in the physical space around or in their head — where 'Now' is.

Some people point to a spot inside their skull, some people point to a location just in front of their nose or their eyes or between their eyebrows.

The partner then asks them to point to where tomorrow is, then next week, next month, six months out, a year out, five years out, ten years out. Each time the person has to identify where — in the physical space around them — they are storing time. The direction, distance out and elevation.

The partner asking the questions maps their responses.

They ask them to point to where yesterday is in their minds, then last week, last month, last year, five years ago, ten years ago.

Some people find it extraordinary to learn that we actually store time in physical space and that our mind space extends beyond our skulls, into the space around us.

The feedback can be equally astounding at first.

Some people store all of time in a sphere of a metre around their head. Some people store 30 years ago 100,000 kilometres behind them. Fifty years in the future is stored 1 million kilometres in front of them.

When someone says they are storing 30 years ago 100,000 kilometres behind them, is that a metaphor or is it true?

In my experience, it is true.

Our metaphysical mind space is absolutely enormous and extends out into the physical realms in all directions. So there is an immediate distinction between the brain, the physical entity and the mind — a metaphysical powerhouse.

In mapping how you store time, you will find that some people program time as a line passing through them. Their future is in front of them in a linear straight line ahead. Their past is behind them in a linear straight line and so time flows through them.

Some people choose to represent time as a left to right line in front of them, with their past out to the left and their future to the right.

When you ask people who have a timeline passing through them, why they chose to program past time behind them, they usually don't know. They may reply that it is logical because their past is behind them, and they are looking into the future.

People who program their timeline in front of them, from left to right, often say that they like to keep an eye on the past because the experience of the past guides them in the future.

People employ different time storage strategies, usually adopted unconsciously. All have merit.

For some people, time curves.

It really doesn't matter how and where you store time, as long as it makes sense for you.

You will occasionally find people who store time randomly. Tomorrow may be in front of them, the day after that may be exactly behind them, five years ago may be six inches in front of them and next month is off behind them at an angle of 40 degrees.

If you program time irregularly, in a confused and disorganised way, it is unlikely that your plans will be logical and smooth flowing.

Even if you did not consciously plan where you store time originally, it is very easy to reorganise your time planning. You can simply reach out, with your eyes closed, grabbing tomorrow and literally placing it where you want it to be in physical space.

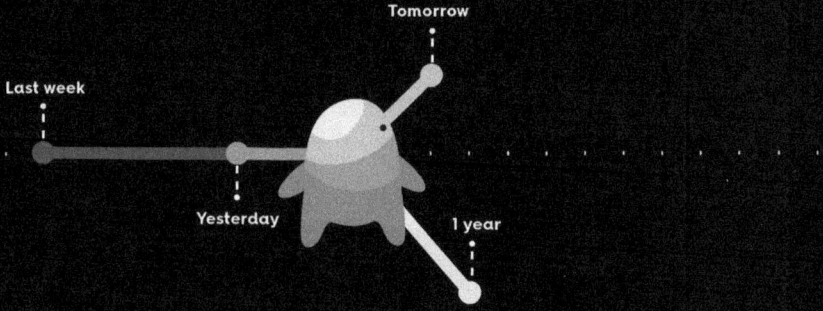

Last week

Tomorrow

Yesterday

1 year

10 years ago · Last year · Last week · Yesterday · Tomorrow · Next week · Next year · 10 years time

10 years ago
Last year
Last week
Yesterday
Now
Tomorrow
Next week
Next year
10 years time

10 years ago
Last year
Last week
Yesterday
Now
Tomorrow
Next week
Next year
10 years time

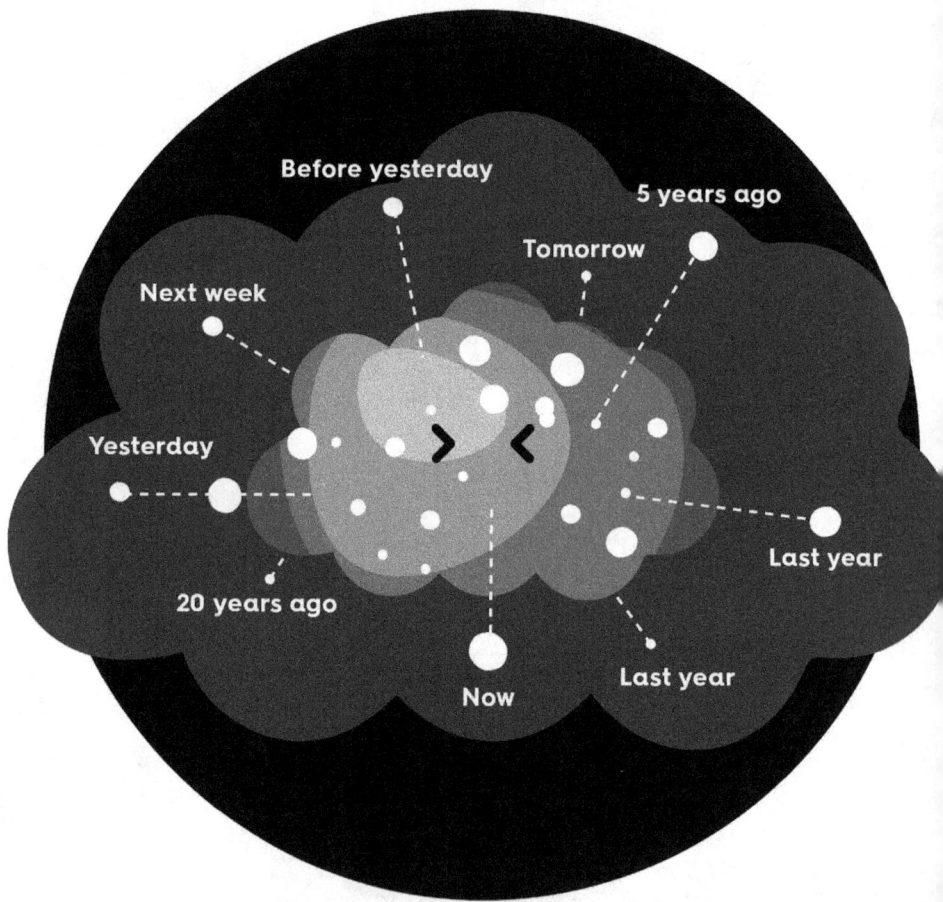

▶ REPROGRAMMING TIME STORAGE

People who have a disorganised time storage system can actually rearrange their spatial time storage system to reprogram their bio-computer. This might sound a little way out — but it has proven a very useful tool to help people improve their planning ability.

If you — or the people in your team — have a poorly organised spatial representation of time, use this tool to reprogram it.

When I first came across this tool, I found that my future went up in front of me, as though I was climbing a mountain. My past was down behind me. I realised that life would be harder if I programmed time this way because, every day, I set out on an uphill climb. So I chose to move my time line. Instead of waking up every day and facing a mountain, every day I now face a down-hill ski run into my future — with my past going up the slope behind me.

The general manager of a large mining company found that he was also climbing up a time mountain. He decided that he too would prefer to move his future downhill and to place his past time going uphill behind him. He rearranged the time storage system in his bio-computer by closing his eyes, reaching for the future in the physical space in front of him and moving it to a downhill position. He rang me three months later to tell me how much easier life had become since changing his time storage system.

We have covered the keys to purpose and vision, passion — and now planning — to ensure you have clear plans of action. You now have some amazing tools to turbo charge the super computer of the mind — to achieve the life you want.

In the next chapter we'll explore tools for managing people because, optimising the performance of other people — so that they are empowered to make the best choices and decisions — is absolutely vital to your success.

FIFTEEN

MANAGING A TEAM

In this chapter we will review a simple management system to ensure that the people you manage are clear about what is required from them as part of your high performance team. This will make it so much easier for you to attract, hire, manage, counsel, correct and appraise each member of your team.

You may also find this management approach useful when working with other people in your community — or even trying to run a house full of kids or teenagers somewhat efficiently!

As a manager, you need to empower people, get them firing on all 16-cylinders and then let them focus their efforts appropriately.

▶ THE CONTRIBUTION CONTRACT

One tool that you can use to help your team achieve outstanding performance lies in developing a Contribution Contract with each team member. The individual Contribution Contract defines what you expect each of them to contribute in achieving personal and team success.

To fire up their 16 BMES cylinders, it is crucial that everybody on your team has 'something significant yet to do'. Their Contribution Contract defines what that is.

At work, this tool is essential. Family life would also probably be far more harmonious if Contribution Contracts were hammered out at the start of each year — so that everyone knew what was expected of them to keep the home show 'on the road'.

There are five steps to developing a contribution contract:

1. **Define their customers**
2. **Define their customers' value criteria**
3. **Define the value criteria of the role — gold medal performance standards**
4. **Define the work to be done**
5. **Add two signatures — Theirs: to be accountable and responsible. Yours: to empower them on all 16-cylinders**

Step 1 — Define their customers

The first step is to identify the customers to whom the team member is in service to.

These could be external customers but also include internal people within your organisation. You, as their manager, are one of their internal customers.

For a House Keeper in a hotel, the hotel guests are his or her external customers. The hotel manager, hotel maintenance and room service supervisors would be their internal customers.

An orchestra Conductor has customers — the audience who come to hear the orchestra play and the musicians who look to him for guidance and instructions.

The first critical point of a Contribution Contract is to make sure that it is customer focused — everybody, everywhere, needs to satisfy a customer.

A customer-focused Contribution Contract will give your people stability and resilience especially during challenging times.

For example, a Receptionist may have four major groups of customers:

➡ **Visitors to reception**

➡ **Incoming calls**

➡ **The organisation's staff**

➡ **His / her manager**

Step 2 — Define the criteria by which their customers assess value

The second step of the Contribution Contract is to clarify the criteria by which each customer is assessing value from your team member's contribution.

If your staff member has a number of customers, it is likely each customer or group of customers may have different value criteria.

In the case of the Receptionist, the customers may have the following value criteria by which they are assessing service and performance:

Contribution Contract

 1 **Define Their Customers**

 2 **Define Their Customers' Value Criteria**

 3 **Define The Value Criteria of the role**
Gold Medal Performance Standards

 4 **Define The Work To Be Done**

- Arrive 8.25am
- Check messages
- Issue visitor passes

1. J.Smith
2. D.O'neil

5 **Add Two Signatures**
Theirs: to be accountable and responsible.
Yours: to empower them on all 16 cylinders

Receptionist Contribution Contract

Your Customers	Their Value Criteria
→ In coming callers	Speed of response in answering the phone, friendliness of tone, skill in directing the call to the right department, clear articulation of any problems or delays to the customer's call
→ Visitors to reception	Speed of service, friendliness, helpful manner, knowledge of company personnel
→ Our staff	Outstanding service ethic, knowledge of company personnel
→ Your manager	Punctuality, outstanding service ethic, adherence to dress code, technical capability

Step 3 — Define Gold Medal Performance

The third of the five steps is to clarify the standard of performance for each of the set of customer's value criteria.

What level of performance will ensure a 'gold medal' from customers?

If the customer is happy, you win the gold. If the customer is not happy and goes somewhere else, there is no silver or bronze medal. You win the lead medal and lose their business.

The question is — what does your staff member have to do to achieve a gold medal in the eyes of the customer?

Staying with our Receptionist example, a gold medal performance for each of their customers' value criteria could be defined as follows:

Receptionist Contribution Contract

Your Customers	Their Value Criteria & Gold Medal Performance
→ In coming callers	**Speed of response in answering the phone** • Phone answered in three rings or less is a gold medal performance. Four rings or more is lead medal – unacceptable **Friendliness of tone** • All calls must be answered in a friendly tone with the words – 'Good morning, xyz Company. This is [name]. How can I help you??' Unfriendliness, irritability, or brusqueness equal a lead medal performance. **Skill in directing the call to the right department** • All calls directed to the correct department first time is gold medal performance. Passing customer calls from department to department represents lead medal performance. **Clear articulation of any problems or delays to the customer's call** • Call transfer problems must always be explained to the customer. For a gold medal performance, the procedures of call on hold must be explained to the customer every time: • 'I will be back to you within a maximum of 30 seconds.' Delays of over 30 seconds response to the customer represents a lead medal performance.

→ **Visitors to reception**	**Speed of service** • Personal attention as soon as possible. Eye contact within 30 seconds if busy, friendly, helpful manner • Warm, friendly, helpful attitude under all levels of pressure and stress **Knowledge of company personnel** • Complete mastery of company phone directory and organisation chart.
→ **Our staff**	**Outstanding service ethic** • Total commitment to providing speedy, accurate service under all levels of pressure and stress **Knowledge of company personnel** • Complete mastery of company phone directory and organisation chart
→ **Your manager**	**Punctual work habits** • Gold medal performance is on time, every time — arrival, breaks, departure. Lateness at the reception desk is a lead medal performance, no excuses **Outstanding service ethic** • Recognition that the customer is always important whether they are angry, rude or unfriendly. 'How may I be of service?' is the only acceptable response. Personal irritability, lack of courtesy, smart remarks are lead medal performance. **Acceptable dress sense** • Presentable business attire is vital. **Technical capability with telephone switchboard** • All facets of switchboard equipment understood and demonstrated. No mistakes, no surprises.

Yes, some of these criteria are subjective, but that's the point. Value is perceived by the customer — so value is subjective. If the customer assesses value around a welcoming smile and friendly tone of voice, then that is what is required — each and every time.

Think back to your early jobs. Would you have found it useful to have a Contribution Contract with your boss that made it clear who your customers were, how your performance would be measured and how you had to perform to consistently win gold medals?

Young and inexperienced people on your team especially need this help.

Step 4 — Work to be done

The fourth step in developing a Contribution Contract is to summarise the work to be done, by your staff member, to achieve gold medal standards in the eyes of their customers.

How much detail needs to go into this section on work to be done? At the very least, there needs to be a list of bullet points summarising the work to be done.

For a younger, more inexperienced team member, it could be useful to set out — in detail — the work to be done.

Contribution Contract — Receptionist

➡ **Work to be done**
➡ **Arrive at 8.25am**
➡ **Be at reception desk with headphones on by 8.30am**
➡ **Switch off overnight answering machine**
➡ **Listen to voice messages and forward to staff**
➡ **Balance the demands of incoming calls and reception arrivals**
➡ **Ensure relief staff in place before taking breaks**
➡ **Notify manager of sickness or absence by 7.30am**
➡ **Activate answer machine before leaving reception at 5.30pm or at any other time when no relief is available**
➡ **Report switchboard problems immediately to service provider**
➡ **Issue visitor passes and record all visitor arrivals in the visitor register**

Having Contribution Contracts makes it so much easier to manage the induction of new people so they quickly learn the basic rules of their role, what is expected of them and how they'll be assessed. Most people want the gold medal!

At home these can be posted on the fridge door.

Step 5 — Two signatures

The fifth step in developing the Contribution Contract is that it requires two signatures.

First, your team member signs that they are accountable and responsible for meeting their customers' value criteria to gold medal standards.

You, as their manager, then sign that you agree to support and empower them to achieve success.

➡ **Staff Signature**
— I agree that I am accountable and responsible to achieve gold medal standards for each of my customers' value criteria.

➡ **Manager Signature**
— I agree that my role is to support and empower you to succeed in your role and to achieve a gold medal standard.

Before we review these tools to assist you in supporting and empowering your people, it is necessary to explore the history of management and to explain the crucial paradox that managers face in developing Contribution Contracts with their people.

▶ THE HISTORY OF MANAGEMENT

To understand management and leadership dilemmas, we need to review the changes in management from the Agrarian age through the Industrial Revolution and into the current Information age — with a rate of change that's making our heads spin.

The Agrarian age

During the Agrarian age, our ancestors were hunter gatherers and then farmers. Most people lived on the land and the rhythm and pace of life were defined by the seasons. They planted in the Spring, their crops grew in the Summer, they harvested in the Autumn and then they ploughed in the Winter. Skills were passed down through families. Trade skills were learned under the apprentice/ journeyman/mastery system we have discussed.

The Industrial age

The Agrarian way of life changed forever when, in 1763, James Watt invented the steam engine. The power of the steam engine — and Bessemer's development of steel production — increased our ability to produce goods and this ushered in the Industrial Revolution. The higher tensile strength of steel beams enabled the construction of large factories that housed the manufacturing machines driven by steam power.

The machines produced goods but needed people to operate them.

So where did the labour come from? People flocked from their farms to work in the factories and so towns grew larger and larger. The people coming from the farms were not educated people.

The business owners that owned the factories required a new type of worker — the Manager. The Manager was needed to tell the workers what to do and make sure the work was done.

In the Agrarian age, the seasons defined the pace of life. Once you have a steam engine, you can run a factory 24 hours a day, seven days a week. The pace of the games of life and business changed forever.

A fundamental principle of the Industrial Revolution was that managers needed to be intelligent and trained to direct worker activity.

They understood what needed to be done in the factory. So Managers managed and workers worked. The education system developed to supply workers with basic primary skills and managers with secondary enhanced skills.

Agrarian Age

90% on the land - labour intensive

Pace:
RHYTHM
OF THE
SEASONS

Industrial Age

Labour/Do

Capiltalists
$$$ Machines

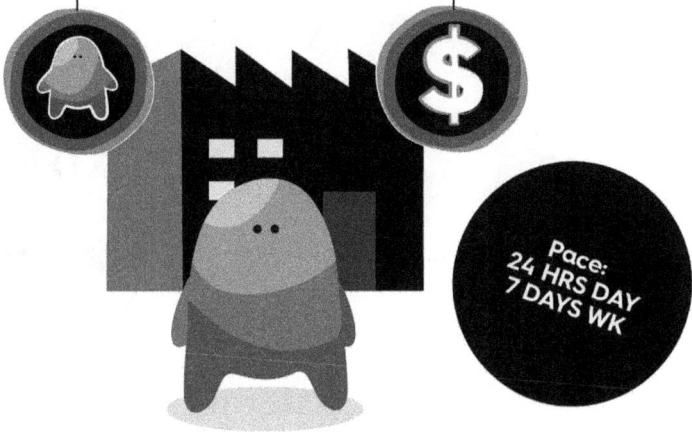

Pace:
24 HRS DAY
7 DAYS WK

Managers / Tell

Information Age

Copper cable ——————→ Glass fibre
                       [Light speed]

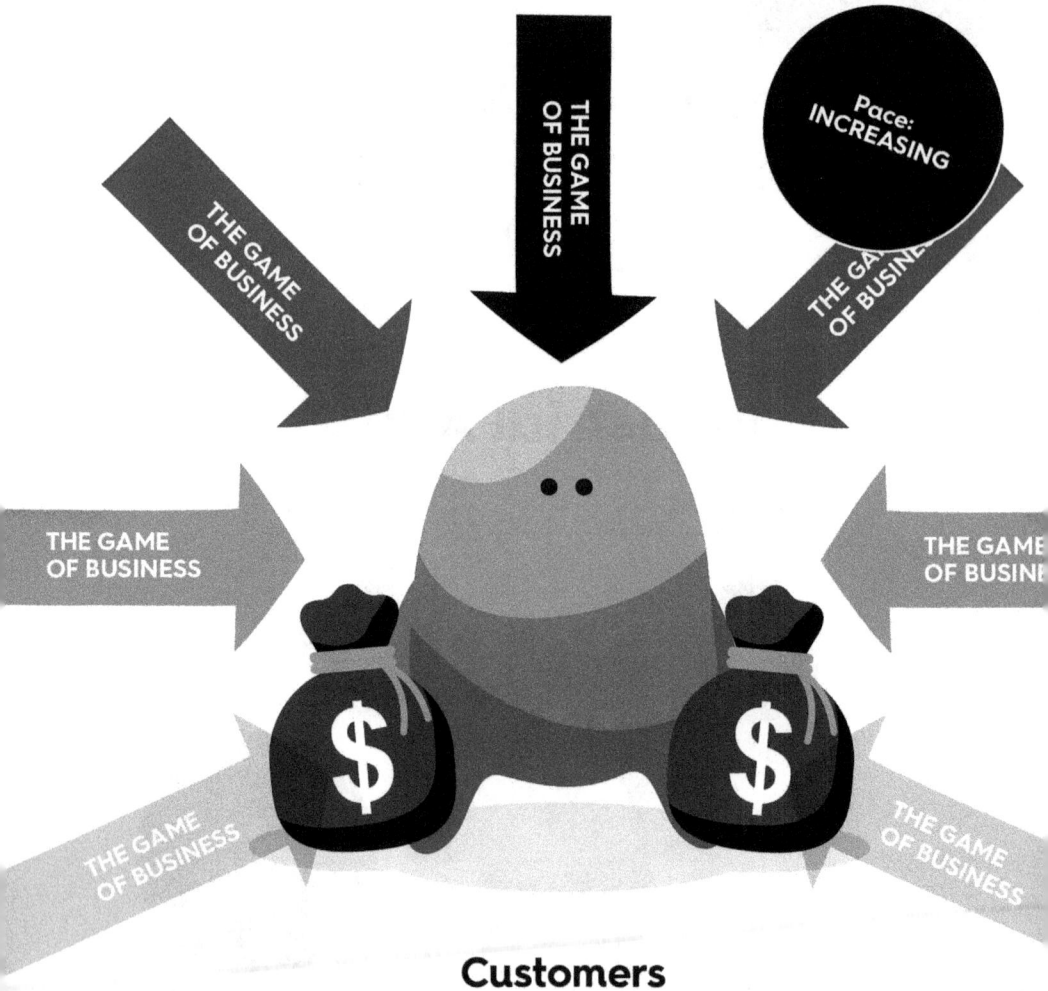

THE GAME OF BUSINESS

Pace:
INCREASING

THE GAME OF BUSINESS

THE GAME OF BUSINESS

THE GAME OF BUSINESS

THE GAME OF BUSINESS

THE GAME OF BUSINESS

THE GAME OF BUSINESS

$

$

Customers

The Information age

We have now moved rapidly beyond the Industrial age into the Information age.

The pace of change is quickening. Manufactured goods account for far less than they used to across world economies that are now more service driven. The endless range of choice has shifted the game of business to a customer focus, customer value, customer loyalty and the creativity to differentiate yourself from the competition.

▶ THE MODERN MANAGEMENT DILEMMA

These changes have created a subtle management dilemma you must be aware of and know how to handle if you are to optimise your life journey skills.

In any enterprise, your people spend more time with your customers than you do. They also know more about your customers on a day-to-day, hour-by-hour basis then you do.

Classical management theory says that you, as the Manager, need to tell your people what to do. In the 21st century, it's impossible for a Manager to create a Team Member's Contribution Contract in isolation. To ensure your team member is firing on all 16-cylinders, it is critical that the Contribution Contract is jointly worked out between you both.

▶ INVOLVE THEIR CUSTOMERS

You will also have to talk to the team member's customers to gain clarity on their value criteria. You can then work with your team member to define Step 4 — the work to be done.

By the time the Contribution Contract is signed, all parties are clear on what their contribution needs to be. When your team member signs they are accountable and responsible for achieving these results, they are signing with their eyes wide open. You, in turn, can then say with integrity — 'We both understand the task ahead of you. My job is to empower you to win gold medals for both of us.' Win / Win.

▶ SUPPORTING AND EMPOWERING YOUR PEOPLE

How do you, as the manager, support and empower your people to sustain 16-cylinder performance? Once the Contribution Contract is clear and both parties know what a gold medal performance looks like, then supporting and empowering your team is simply a question of assisting them in three areas:

1. **Able to** — Is your team member able to do the job with adequate skills and abilities?

2. **Want to** — Do they want to do the job — are they motivated?

3. **Chance to** — Are you allowing them to perform at gold medal standards by providing excellent systems and a success oriented win/win culture?

This progressive management system is summarised in the following diagram. The Contribution Contract defines what is expected.

This is important. Life skills mastery requires that you make the right choices.

When faced with a person who is not performing, there are five questions to ask:

1. **Do they understand the game — 'let's achieve the vision'?**
2. **Do they know the rules**
   – their personal contribution?
3. **Are they able to play the game to win**
   – skills and abilities?
4. **Do they have the chance to play the game**
   – supported with good systems and culture?
5. **Do they want to play the game**
   – are they motivated?

With these five questions, we can now explore approaches that will assist you to support and empower each person on your team.

Want to

Does your staff member want to work on your team and achieve the vision? Are they motivated?

You now have the tools for trust and rapport building in your toolkit, you understand their values, their DISC needs and fears, their domains of balance, their life journey this far and their level of enthusiasm.

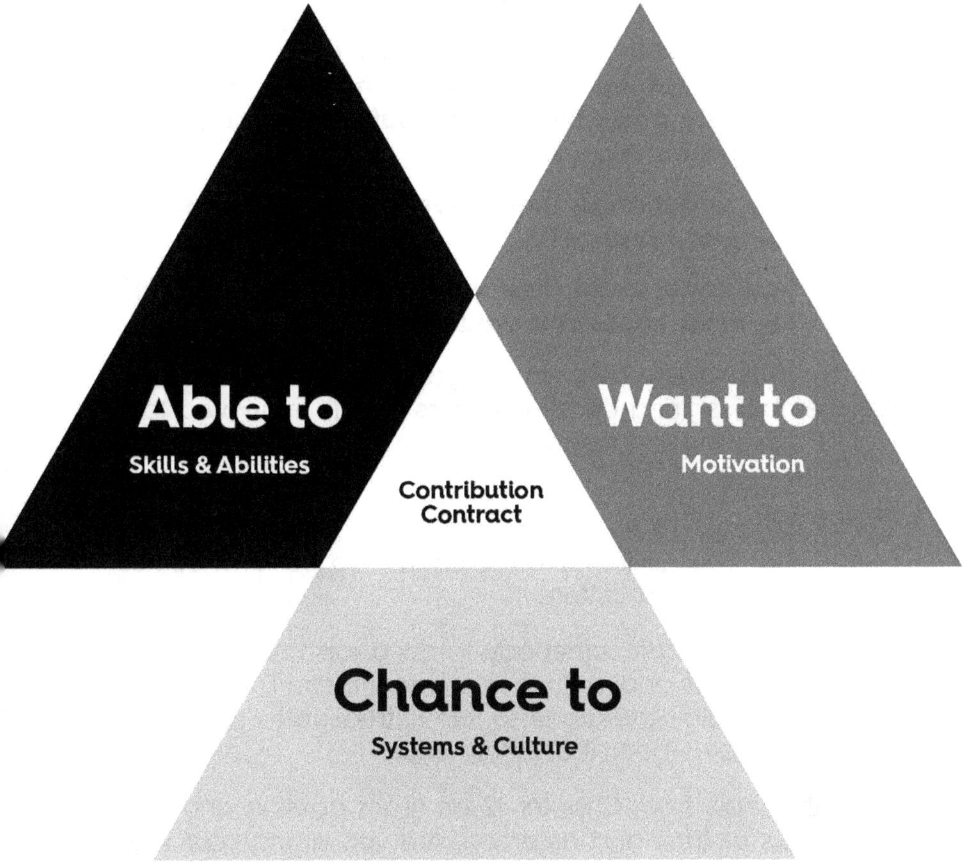

Able to
Skills & Abilities

Want to
Motivation

Contribution
Contract

Chance to
Systems & Culture

- ➡ **Do they have a clear sense of their personal journey and purpose?**

- ➡ **Have they worked out the win/win exchange of working on your team?**

- ➡ **Have they a clear understanding of what it is they're giving and gaining that's preparing them for their longer term life journey?**

- ➡ **Do they have an explicit personal growth contract with you as we discussed in Chapter 10.**

- ➡ **Do you understand their preferred DISC graphic equaliser settings, so that you can reach out and consistently press their needs button and avoid pressing their fears button?**

- ➡ **Do you understand their priorities across the seven domains of balance?**

- ➡ **Do you understand their values hierarchy and their single, most important value?**

All of these tools are available to you to ensure that your team member is firing on all cylinders and is motivated to work towards achieving the vision.

Chance to

Ensuring that your team have the chance to perform comes down to systems and culture.

It is very unfair to ask somebody to do a job and not provide adequate systems and culture to support them. Denying someone the chance to play the game to win is treason to the spirit within and demonstrates poor leadership skills.

Review the tools from Chapter 12 on team passion and the culture tools of trust and assertion. Are you giving your team the chance to perform at gold medal standards?

Many performance problems are caused by sloppy, inefficient systems but, because most of us are not trained in systems analysis, we miss the root cause of the sloppy system and then blame the effect — the person not performing or making the mistake. Does your team have well organised systems supporting them so that they can be flexible and creative in their work? It is possible you are not fully across the detail of how your systems do or don't support your team, because you may not be immersed in them every day.

Sit down with each team member and say something to this effect:

→ **'Now that we have the Contribution Contract in place, and we've both signed it, my job is to support and empower you. I will do that by consistently coming back to these three questions.**

→ **Are you able to, do you want to, and do you have the chance to perform to the gold medal standards we agreed?**

→ **In the area of want to, if we have performance issues to discuss, I will be using the keys to passion to make sure I can help you stay motivated.**

→ **When we analyse the chance to, let us jointly review the support systems. I want to make sure the systems are there to support you to achieve gold medal performance.**

→ **We need to be clear on which of your support systems are well organised and efficient — and which are sloppy and need improvement.'**

List of Support Systems for the Receptionist

→ **Reception desk — safe, comfortable and efficient**

→ **Switchboard — works effectively**

→ **Computer / Printer — operating**

→ **High Quality Reception Chair**

→ **Phone Directory — out of date**

→ **Organisation Charts — sloppy & out of date**

→ **Relief staff for breaks — unclear**

Once you both agree on the support systems and their current state, develop a set of action plans to get the systems to a gold medal standard. Will you be able solve all your system problems in a day? Highly unlikely.

However, as long as your team is aware of where the systems are letting them down, then you can adjust your Contribution Contract expectations accordingly. As the systems are improved to gold medal standards, the gold medal performance can be expected and achieved every time. With the 'chance to' box ticked — spirit enthusiasm increases markedly.

Able to

Having used your 'want to' and 'chance to' empowerment tools, you have another area of managerial support to address.

If your team members 'want to' and have the 'chance to' perform, are they 'able to' perform? Do they have the skills and proper training?

You need a considered approach and strategy for reviewing current and required skill levels.

It can be challenging to communicate to a team member that they are not quite as 'able to' do the job as they think they are. They need the feedback of course, but good leadership demands that you are mindful of their self-esteem. No one likes implied criticism.

Known strengths

The best approach for reviewing skills, as the table below shows, is to talk to your team member about their known strengths first. That is a good way to start an 'able to' review — it reassures people and makes them feel at ease.

'Let's look at your strengths — they are formidable so let's make a list of them.'

Unknown strengths

Once you have covered their known strengths, it's a good time to talk about their unknown strengths.

'There may be an area where you are not aware how strong you are. I want to recognise the sense of integrity that you bring to the team is highly valued by myself and senior management and your team members.'

It's possible that people do not recognise some of the strengths they have.

Highlighting them in the 'able to' review boosts their feelings of self-worth and self-esteem. This can prepare them to be more open for the next two review areas.

A Known Strengths

B Unknown Strengths

C Known Improvement Opportunities

D Unknown Improvement Opportunities

Known improvement opportunities

'We've agreed in the Contribution Contract that Reception is open and operating from 8.30am. There have been a few occasions over the past month where Reception wasn't operating until 8.45am. This is not gold medal performance so let's discuss it and see how we can ensure consistency around this'.

It is entirely possible that their performance is being undermined because of a genuine reason in the area of 'want to' or 'chance to'. You now have the skill or ability gap on the table for continued discussion and correction.

Unknown improvement opportunities

'There is an area of your performance that I need to bring to your attention. The team members who cover Reception when you're on a break are getting frustrated with the length of your breaks. In one instance you were half an hour late back from your lunch break, and in another, you took a 45 minute break at morning tea, which is meant to be 20 minutes. This meant that one colleague was late for an important meeting and another one missed an important deadline. You may not be aware of this problem, so this is a good opportunity to address it.'

Because you have focused first on their strengths, your team member will be better able to handle a more challenging discussion.

Remember that the voice of the ego is always chattering to defend us — 'she should try doing what I have to do. I'd like to see her manage non-stop calls and visitors AND sales people booking meeting rooms for clients.'

Everyone has the voice of ego. The ego's job is to defend us so our self-esteem is not crushed into oblivion. There is a communication hierarchy: truth, justify, blame, deny, quit.

Knowing this may help you and your team member to focus on the reality of the situation and avoid digressing into justification, blame and denial of the performance issues.

Talk through the 'able to' review using the grid to draw out the unknown improvement opportunities. Emphasise the gold medal performance that is required and, together, analyse any action steps required to bring them up to speed. Keep reminding your team member;

'My job is to empower you to do your job to an excellent standard. You have agreed on your contribution to our vision achievement and this is the performance level that you need to achieve — the gold medal / ten out of ten performance. If the motivation, systems and culture are giving you every chance to succeed, then we need to look at your capability. These are the 'Unknown Improvement Opportunities' that we need to discuss today. They stand between you and gold medal performance. In your Contribution Contract I agreed to support and empower you and make you a winner, so we need to address these issues even if it's challenging. Does this make sense, what are your thoughts?'

Once you have talked to your team member using this model, it should make sense, however uncomfortable you both are discussing it. Keep it factual and positive.

▶ MANAGING PEOPLE

Clearly, your team will have a range of abilities and levels of motivation. Drawing the best from each of them will require flexibility in your management approach.

The following diagram shows how to vary your management emphasis.

If you review the diagram, you can see 'want to' on one axis, 'able to' on the other axis and 'chance to' underpins everything. Without well-organised, efficient systems, your people will not be able to consistently perform to gold medal standards. So 'chance to' under-pins everything.

The diagram provides four defined quadrants which represent the four types of people you may need to manage. Life journey skills mastery requires a different management approach for each type of person.

Low able to / high want to

A person may score quite low in terms of able to, because they are lacking skills and experience. Yet they have very high want to, because their motivation is strong. Once the enthusiasm and motivation is high, regular coaching and training will get them there.

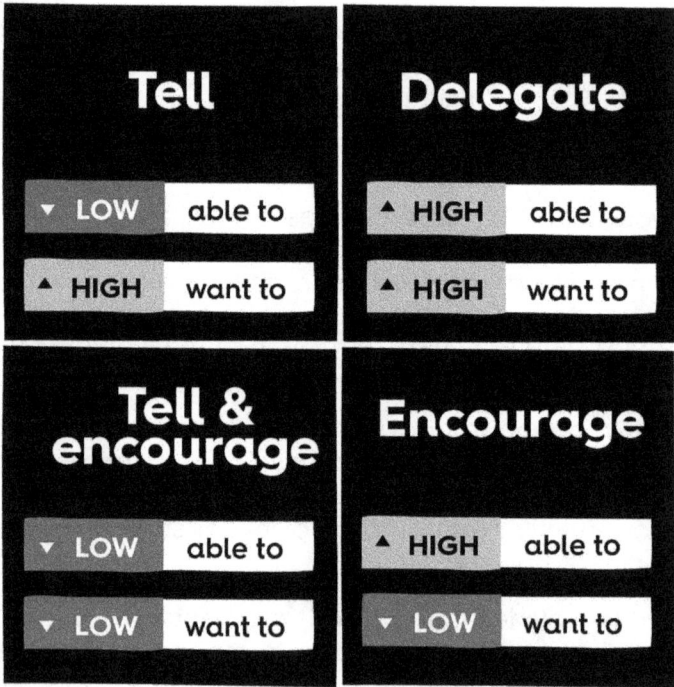

Section 4 of their Contribution Contract, work to be done, needs to be quite detailed. Ask them to tackle the current problem, define an action plan and then come back to you for discussion and approval before proceeding.

There's no doubt that training and mentoring team members can be time consuming but the ROI is definitely worth it. Plus it is really rewarding to watch people grow and develop.

Low able to / low want to

These team members are neither able to nor want to do the job and this presents a real problem for you.

They need to be managed with detailed instructions on how to do the job and you also have to give them constant support and encouragement to motivate them.

This of course can drain your own energy and enthusiasm, but remember, everyone has potential to step up. They could even prove to be a real gem. It may be poor management, systems, culture — or even personal issues — that has shut down their 16-cylinders. See if you can get to the root of the problem and work on helping and motivating them.

Your responsibility is to help them fire up again — so give them a chance by doing the following:

➡ **Set up their Contribution Contract.**

➡ **Give them a detailed Section 4 on work to be done.**

➡ **Analyse their training gaps and develop an action plan to close them.**

➡ **Work through the want to, the motivation and passion tools from Chapter 10 to help them fire up on all 16-cylinders.**

➡ **Make it clear you have a team vision to achieve and that they play a vital role in achieving that vision.**

High able to / low want to

These people are quite able to, but they are not motivated, they don't want to perform to gold medal standards. With the passion tools you now have at your disposal, you can now deal with these difficulties. These team members need a supportive, encouraging management style to help them.

You can either support and re-motivate them — or clarify if indeed they are a square peg in a round hole. Maybe they're in the wrong job and need to find another team.

You need to make it clear to these team members that the vision will only be achieved with a motivated team. Don't tolerate the victim game but do help them, because the spark of spirit can always be rekindled.

So give it everything you've got to help them fire up and re-motivate themselves.

High able to / high want to

With the people who have both ability and personal motivation, you can delegate more. Because they are capable, experienced, self-starters, Section 4 of their Contribution Contract on 'work to be done' needs only be a few summary bullet points.

You need to agree when you are going to have regular check point meetings with them to review progress.

Delegation does not mean abdication. You need to have agreed progress meetings as the other sections of the Contribution Contract are just as important.

Some managers find the 'old hands' very resistant to the introduction of the discipline of Contribution Contracts:

➡ **'We've been doing this with our eyes shut for years. Why do we suddenly need Contribution Contracts? You know I can deliver. Trust me and spend your time on the younger ones. They need your help — not me.'**

Your answer is simple –

➡ **'You know every competitor is after business, so unless we improve our systems and formally focus on the customers as a team discipline, yesterday's gold medal standard only gets us a lead medal tomorrow.'**

➡ **'The bar keeps going up. I need your help as an Influencer so that everyone can see we're serious about gold medal performance. These Contribution Contracts are a critical part of achieving our team vision.'**

➡ **'I really need your active support on this one.'**

▶ APPRAISALS

Another important use of the Contribution Contract comes at appraisal time. You need to have a major appraisal with each of your team members, at least once a year and, in this era of rapid change, you probably need a second shorter appraisal every six months.

You can now appraise against the performance agreed in the Contribution Contract.

With the able to / want to / chance to support and empowerment model in place, you can talk that through with your team member.

A Contribution Contract, with Section 1 listing the customers (internal and external), provides the format for 360 degree feedback. This involves feedback on performance from internal customers — who may be subordinates, peers and superiors — and from external customers.

The Contribution Contract focuses on specific gold medal winning feedback. It is so much easier to review strengths and improvement opportunities against this framework.

▶ HIRING PEOPLE

Hiring the right people can be a real challenge and takes significant time from a busy schedule. Having a clear Contribution Contract for a role makes advertising that much easier. You know the person you are looking for.

A Contribution Contract is far more powerful than a job description or a series of key performance indicators (KPIs).

Why? There's a great quote from Einstein — 'Sooner or later, we realise that the highest calling on the planet is to be of service to our fellow man.'

A job description rarely speaks to the spirit within. Remember, nobody is looking for a job, everyone is looking for a game. When hiring people, discovering what they would like to do in the long term can be very useful. One great tool is to offer a personal growth contract to the candidate. They can then link the motivation of joining your team — and helping realise your vision — with the motivation for their own life journey.

Use the $25m dollar game we've discussed earlier.

Able to
Skills & Abilities

Want to
Motivation

Contribution Contract

Chance to
Systems & Culture

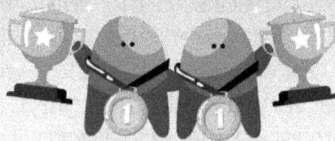

Say to the candidate — 'If you had twenty five million dollars what would you do with your life?' The reason for asking the candidate is to develop a sense of where they are heading. Do they have a powerful sense of life direction? This knowledge serves two purposes. First, it tells you the calibre of person, the spirit within you are dealing with. Secondly, it gives you a hiring hook.

I remember one job candidate who said, 'If I had 25 million dollars, I would move to the country and grow avocados.' I thought to myself, 'Oh well, she seemed a good candidate, but she is not for my team. There is no powerful motivator to encourage a personal growth contract.'

To test her before ending the interview, I said to her, 'Just assume you had been living in the country for ten years. Is that where you really want to live for the rest of your life?'

She said, 'Oh no, I wouldn't stay there all my life.'

So I asked her what she would do then and she said, 'I would come back to the city' and she then gave me a detailed description of the way she would like to be of service to humanity. I asked her, 'What sort of qualities will you need to achieve that long term goal?'

She thought about it and we discussed her growth needs to be the person worthy of attaining her life journey service goals.

I then said, 'Here's the deal. If you join us (because don't forget, good candidates usually have several alternative job offers), I will expect you to put in a 100 per cent effort to achieve gold medal performance in the areas specified in your contribution contract. I will support and empower you to make sure you achieve consistent gold medal performance standards. I will also further empower you by increasing your skills in the areas you will need on your longer term life journey'.

That is a Personal Growth Contract offer that your competitors (who are also trying to attract this candidate) are unlikely to make because they don't have this tool.

Using these empowerment models can be powerful in attracting the right people to your team. Most people want to play the games of life and business on 16-cylinders and there are relatively few 16-cylinder opportunities out there.

Offering them a 16-cylinder environment coupled with life journey growth (explicitly stated) will give you a great edge to attract and retain the best people.

▶ USING THE LAW OF GRAVITY TO ATTRACT CALIBRE CANDIDATES

To assist you in understanding how to attract the right people to your team, there is a generalised principle of physics we can use here to explain a powerful law of metaphysics.

Newton's law of gravity states that the force of attraction — 'F' — between two physical bodies is a function of 'G' — the gravitational constant — multiplied by 'M1' — the mass of one body — multiplied by 'M2' — the mass of the other — divided by the square of the distance — 'd' — between them.

Because this law of physical gravity is a generalised principle, it holds true throughout the physical universe. Gravity is the force that holds the physical universe of planets, stars and galaxies in place.

Equally, a force of metaphysical gravity is always present as a metaphysical generalised principle. Everyone has metaphysical mass related to the state of their mind, emotions and spirit and the way they live.

Someone with limited, fearful thinking, living with no integrity, will have a small, unattractive metaphysical mass. Someone who is sharp and alert, emotionally alive and living to high standards of integrity and service will have a larger metaphysical mass.

Because you, your team and your vision have a certain combined metaphysical mass, you need to explore the effects this law is having on your business.

What sort of people are you attracting? The laws of gravitational metaphysics affect the people and customers you'll attract.

So the larger, the shinier, the brighter you make your team, work environment, culture and vision, the more likely you are to attract the calibre candidates you need to achieve your vision. The weakest force exerted by your vision on your team is the day you first draw it.

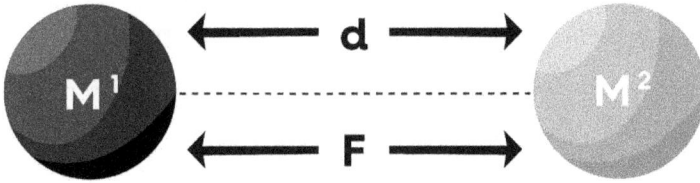

$$F = \frac{G \times M^1 \times M^2}{d^2}$$

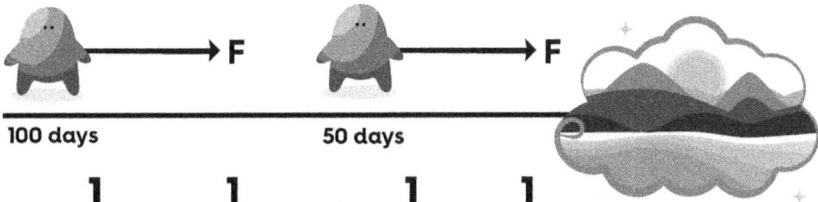

100 days

50 days

$$F = \frac{1}{100^2} = \frac{1}{10,000} \qquad F = \frac{1}{50^2} = \frac{1}{2,500}$$

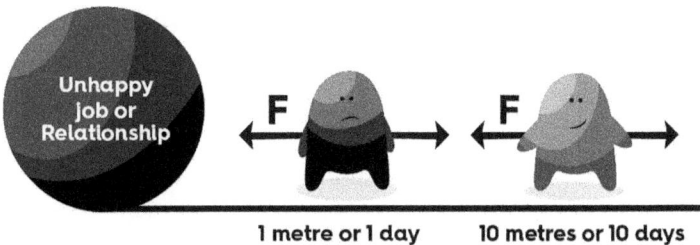

Unhappy job or Relationship

1 metre or 1 day

10 metres or 10 days

$$F = \frac{1}{1} \qquad F = \frac{1}{10^2} = \frac{1}{100}$$

The metaphysical gravity of attraction between your team and the vision increases with each day of action.

The metaphysics of leaving

The law of metaphysical gravity also shows that the toughest step in walking away from an unhappy job or relationship — is the first.

One metre out — the force pulling the person back is one over one — squared and equals one. Ten metres out, the force pulling back drops to one over ten — squared and is 100 times weaker.

It's twice as tough because the pull towards their preferred future — or new partner — is the weakest with the first step as the previous diagram shows. If one of your people wants to leave your team to expand their life journey but is finding the decision hard, show them the diagram.

If they do need to move on, help them leave. Like the journeymen in the Middle Ages, they can always return later with a whole new world of experiences to bring to your team's vision achievement.

▶ SUMMARY

Now you have tools to provide your people with:

➡ **Purpose and vision**

➡ **Passion, motivation and enthusiasm**

➡ **Plans of action**

With their Contribution Contracts, you also have a systematic approach to coaching them to high performance by ensuring that — at all times — they are:

➡ **Able to**

➡ **Want to**

➡ **Have the Chance to perform**

In the next chapter, we need to explore the fourth critical key to success — persistence. This is a vital tool because the aliens of resistance will show up and you must prevail and succeed. Persistence is essential in business as in life!

PART FIVE:

PERSISTENCE

SIXTEEN

THE POWER OF PERSISTENCE

'The most important characteristics you need to succeed in business are resilience, determination and persistence.'
KARREN BRADY

▶ WINNING THE GAME

Life mastery is developed by overcoming obstacles and gaining experience in achieving worthwhile vision and goals.

To achieve consistently outstanding results, the ability to demonstrate the fourth success principle is the great divide between the gold medal winners and the rest.

It is summarised in one word — persistence — from the Latin 'per sistere' — to stand firm throughout.

Persistence is the fourth success key from Think and Grow Rich.

▶ DEFEATING THE RESISTANCE

Why is this? Because your enemy is resistance, from the Latin 're sistere' — to stand against you. On your life journey I have no doubt you have met the resistance enemy often.

The Scottish poet Robert Burns said:

'The best laid schemes o' mice and men gang aft aglay.'

Rough translation — shit happens!

At work, resistance can come in many forms — an off-spec product for a crucial customer, an unexpected IT crash, a competitor price drop or new campaign, the resignation of a key staff member or a failure to meet deadlines — on and on it goes.

The list of challenges that can wear down people's enthusiasm and staying power is endless.

The enemy is alive and well. The issue with resistance is not whether it's going to show up to stop you.

The issue is what you — and the people around you — do when it does show up.

The quality of persistence is vital, and you must ensure everyone has powerful strategies to beat the enemy.

This chapter explores the tools you and your team need to minimise the chance of the enemy of resistance winning.

▶ SYSTEMS ARE YOUR FRIEND

Your primary weapon in developing the power of persistence is a focus on systems.

Many resistance aliens can be defeated by increasing your awareness and understanding of the systems supposed to support and empower your people.

Examples of systems

Systems are an organised approach to achieving more efficient and effective activity.

In the 1660s, accountants in Venice invented the general ledger as a systematic way of recording business transactions.

Traffic lights and white lines are systems designed to move the traffic around without too many mistakes or accidents.

Many different systems support your team — computer systems, quality control systems, telecommunication systems, communication systems. We are surrounded by systems.

At home you may have the laundry system, the pantry system, the drop off pick up system. They are all systems, designed to make your day, week — and life — flow as smoothly as possible.

The need for good systems

One of the best proponents of systems analysis was an American named W. Edwards Deming.

After the Second World War, he thought a competitive advantage in the post-war global market would be systematic measurement, communication, and cooperation.

He first visited Japan in 1946 under the auspices of the Economic and Scientific section of the US Department of War. In the ensuing years, he contributed to Japanese industry as they rebuilt their economy.

97 per cent of mistakes and problems originate from poor systems

Deming is reported to have said that 97% of all mistakes and problems originate from sloppy, inefficient systems. And we now know that a mistake is a withdrawal from the trust account.

Usually, a mistake appears to be caused by a team member.

Although the cause of the mistake looks like it's a person, the real cause is almost always in the system supporting — or not supporting — the team member. The apparent poor performance of the person is an effect from the root cause which is a sloppy support system.

If you've ever tackled a blocked drain, you will know that the blockage is the effect. The cause can be the roots of a tree many meters away.

To maintain a high-performance team, when mistakes or problems occur, always review the systems supporting your team. Ninety-seven per cent of the time, the root cause of the problem will lie in the systems.

Systems education

The problem in tackling systems is that most of us get little training in systems analysis.

That's why we don't discern the problem. We only see the effect, the person apparently making the mistake. We are just not trained to spot the underlying root cause — the often invisible, sloppy, inefficient system. That was Deming's point.

Life and business mastery requires that you focus on systems analysis. Why?

Because poor systems are the source of 97 per cent of mistakes and problems that can crush the enthusiasm of the spirit within.

This is vital at work and, equally important at home and in your community.

▶ KAIZEN

With Deming's help, the Japanese industry developed the concept of Kaizen — constant and never-ending systems and quality improvement.

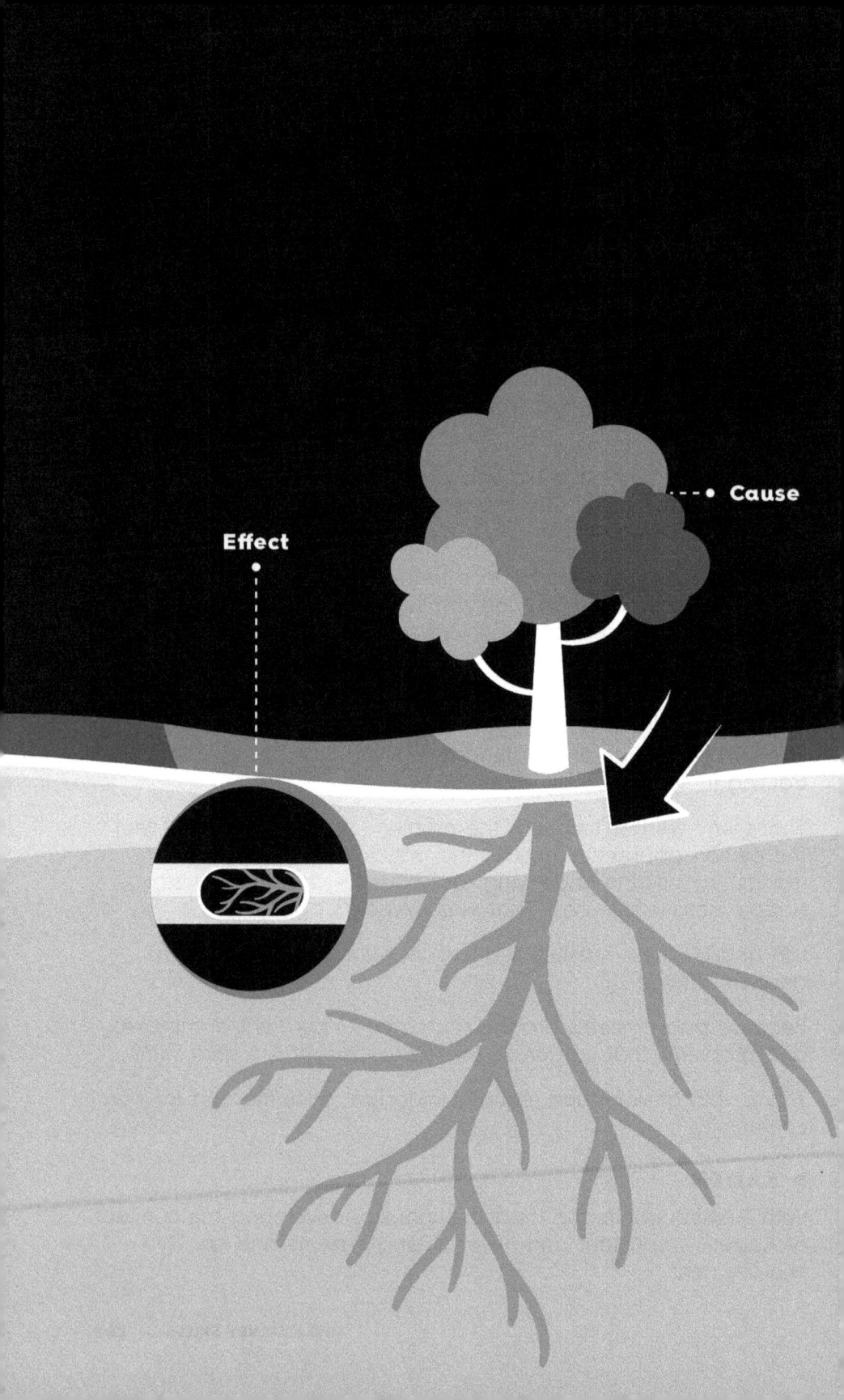

For instance, the original idea for the Sony Walkman came from Sony co-founder, Akio Morita, when he saw that his daughter Naoko was very keen to have music around her everywhere she went. His partner, Masara Ibuka, also wanted a portable unit and complained about the weight of early Sony portable tape recorders.

Initial production of a portable, light-weight unit and headphones was quite an engineering challenge. The Walkman improved through many models, because the Japanese realised that you could not reach the perfect product in one iteration. It was necessary to improve step by step — Kaizen.

Kaizen is constant and never-ending improvement. If you want your people to have strong empowering culture and the ability to show resilience and persistence, you have to employ the principle of never-ending improvement to your systems.

Your top six systems

List the top six systems that your team performance depends on.

They might be computing systems, scheduling systems or sales systems. Just take a few minutes to note them down.

Now ask yourself which systems are somewhat inefficient and not supporting your people to achieve gold medal performance?

▶ FLUID FLOW — LAMINAR VERSUS TURBULENT

To understand the importance of systems for your team in terms of culture, resilience, passion and persistence, let's review another law of physics and the relevant law of metaphysics.

Take the example of fluid flow. Let's look at the difference between lamina flow and turbulent flow.

Liquid pumped through a smooth, well-formed pipe displays very efficient lamina flow.

Lamina flow is when the components of a liquid or gas are moving smoothly and efficiently down a pipe. A laminar flow pattern optimises flow.

If a snag is introduced to the inside surface of the pipe, then the liquid will break into turbulent flow. Turbulent flow is much less efficient.

Flow rates drop by 20-40% once lamina flow changes to turbulent flow.

High levels of passion and persistence are critical if your team is to flow in a lamina format — proceeding smoothly and supported by excellent systems.

This law of fluid flow should sound alarm bells. Inefficient systems can have a massive negative effect on your team culture — and on the team's ability to demonstrate persistence and achieve high performance results.

Working on your systems can provide a major ROI in your efforts to hone a resilient, high performance team success culture.

Systems analysis is just as relevant at home as it is at work.

Faced with this major source of resistance, life mastery requires a systems focus everywhere.

You won't ever need to worry about external competition if your own, self-generated competition — below optimal systems — cripples your team.

Check your top six systems and go to your Commitments Register. Note down what can be done to tighten up your inefficient systems.

▶ SYSTEMS ACCOUNTABILITY

In every organisation everybody has a tale to tell of inefficient and sloppy systems. Everyone knows which systems are failing them.

Systems analysis is the first challenge.

Working out who is accountable for a system can be the second major challenge — because often responsibility for systems spans several functional areas in a company.

Because most of us are not trained in systems analysis, we cannot see the problems in the systems. So functional teams likely will not easily spot the cross-functional systems problems.

To overcome resistance, you must tackle this issue by forming cross-functional systems analysis teams.

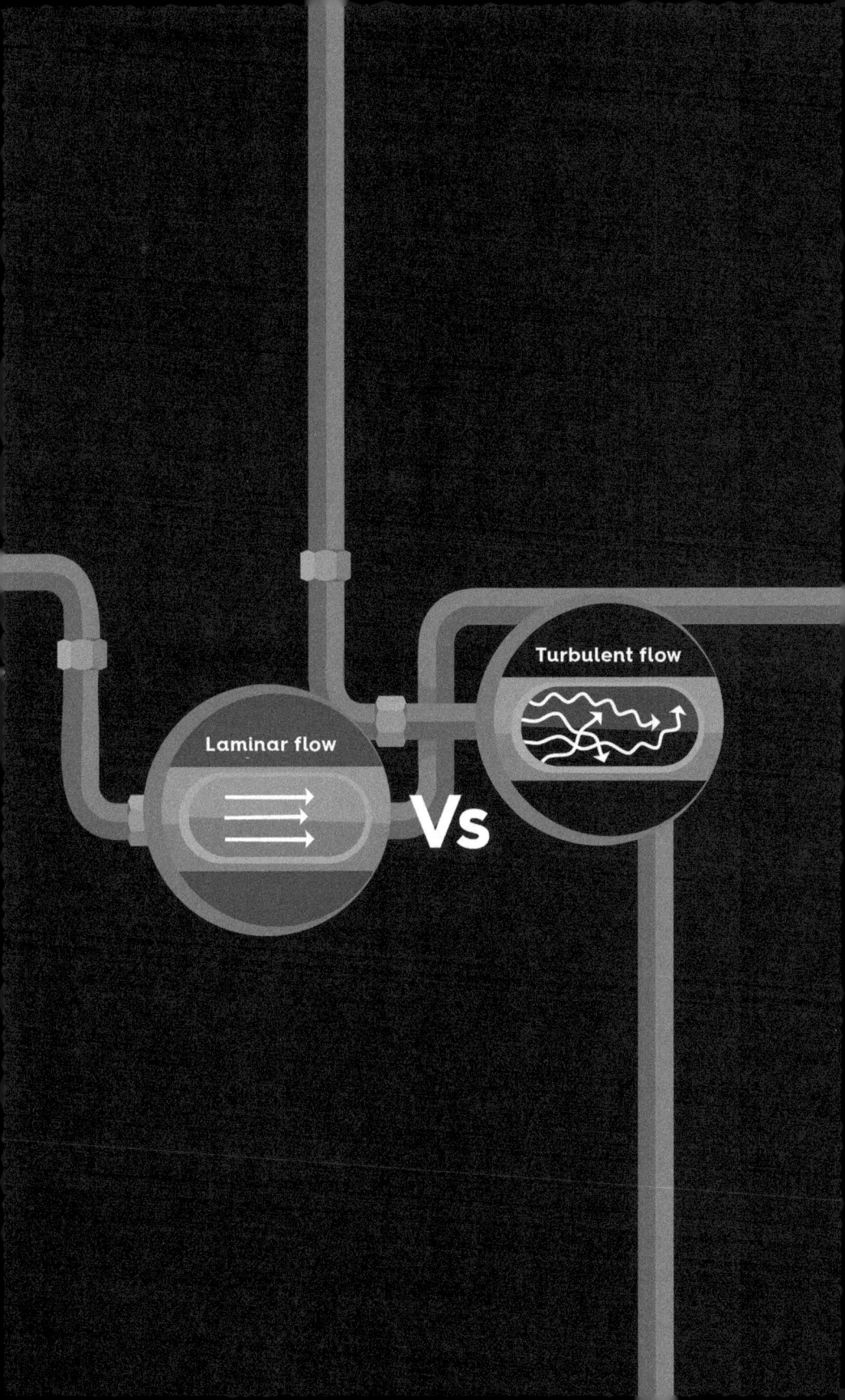
Laminar flow

Vs

Turbulent flow

If you leave it to 'someone else', the resistance aliens thrive. You need unreasonable champions to fix your sloppy systems, people who are prepared to take on the challenges of inefficient systems. It can be a real battle needing tenacity and passion.

Boiled frogs

You may have heard of the famous experiment of the boiled frog: if you put a frog in cold water in a pot and heat the water up quickly, the frog will jump out. However, if you put a frog in cold water and warm the water very slowly, the frog does not notice and as the temperature rises, the frog drifts into unconsciousness and finally dies.

We are often blind to our systems issues. The resistance aliens have crept up and are slowly 'boiling us alive'.

Alien of the month

With our clients, we often have an 'alien of the month' focus. We run a systems analysis around the question — what's not working?

I highly recommend it for your next team meeting. You can preface the review of what's not working with an upbeat review of what's working really well.

Put your team's list of poor systems in order of priority — and then choose the highest priority system to work on.

Make that system the resistance 'alien of the month' and develop a flame thrower strategy to fix the problem. Specify what has to be done, by whom by when, to improve the system to gold medal standards.

Use the PERT graphical planning technique to work back from the end result — what happened just before that? This will provide a plan to ensure the specific system is improved permanently.

Excellent systems are a key competitive advantage.

'When people understand the entire system, there is something about the human spirit that spontaneously aspires to be competent and succeed.'
W EDWARDS DEMING

Ohm's law

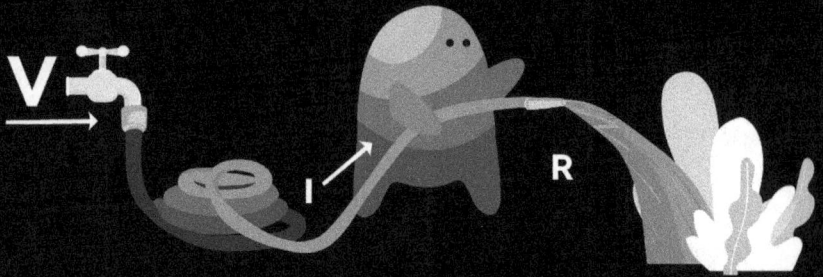

V →

I

R

Water I = V / R

Energy & enthusiasm

I →

I = V / R

▶ PHYSICS AND METAPHYSICS OF PERSISTENCE

When analysing your systems, it is logical to start with the physical systems that support your team. However, that's not enough, don't stop there. To maximise persistence, you need to look at the metaphysics affecting the team.

Ohm's law

As we've discussed, the laws of physics are replicated in the laws of metaphysics.

One law of physics very useful in improving team and personal persistence is Ohm's Law. Georg Ohm worked with electricity and his law is usually expressed as:

➡ $V = I * R$

'V' the voltage equals 'I' the current multiplied by 'R' the resistance.

For our purposes, the law is best expressed as:

➡ $I = V / R$

Where the current 'I' equals 'V' the voltage divided by 'R' the resistance.

In the diagram, the current flowing through the wire 'I' is a function of 'V' the voltage of the battery — which is like the pressure in the battery pushing the electrons down the wire. 'R' is the resistance of the filament in the light bulb.

To increase the current 'I' flowing through the wire, you either have to increase 'V' the voltage, or reduce the resistance 'R' of the filament. Either way there is an increase in the flow of current 'I'.

Ohm's law is equally applicable to the physics of the hose you use to water the garden.

'I' now equals the flow of water through the hose pipe, 'V' is the water pressure and 'R' is the resistance of the spray nozzle.

To increase 'I' the flow of water through the hose pipe, you have two choices: increase the water pressure 'V' or reduce the resistance 'R' of the spray nozzle by changing from a fine spray to a strong jet.

Ohm's Law is a law of physics yet it equally applies in the law of metaphysics.

Suppose you have a good team, but there is a problem with persistence.

You've defined the purpose. You have developed a vision. You have clear plans of action. The graphical PERT planning charts are up on the wall.

You've spent time working out where each team member sits on the DISC profile. Contribution Contracts are in place.

You've done everything you can to fire up each team member on all 16-cylinders — and yet you are still having problems.

You need more energy and more enthusiasm in your team. They don't seem able to sustain their enthusiasm when problems arise. They lack persistence — the ability to stand firm throughout. What do you do?

Try applying Ohm's law to the metaphysics of your team.

If 'I' equals the energy and enthusiasm flowing through your team, — which is a measure of their ability to persist — what is 'V'? 'V' is the power of your team vision. To increase team enthusiasm, you need to increase the power of the vision that's motivating your team to move forwards towards an exciting, co-created future.

Perhaps the vision is as good as you can do. So what else can you do to improve enthusiasm, energy and persistence capability?

Ohm's law indicates that — to increase enthusiasm and persistence further — you have to reduce resistance 'R'. On a team, what does it mean to have resistance in the metaphysics?

The law of entrainment

We need to turn to another generalised law of physics: the law of entrainment, because the law of entrainment gives you your first clue to resistance on your team.

In 1665 a Dutch scientist, Christian Huygens, discovered that if two cuckoo clocks are placed side by side on a wall, within the space of a few days, the pendulums swing in a synchronised manner, even though they are not connected physically.

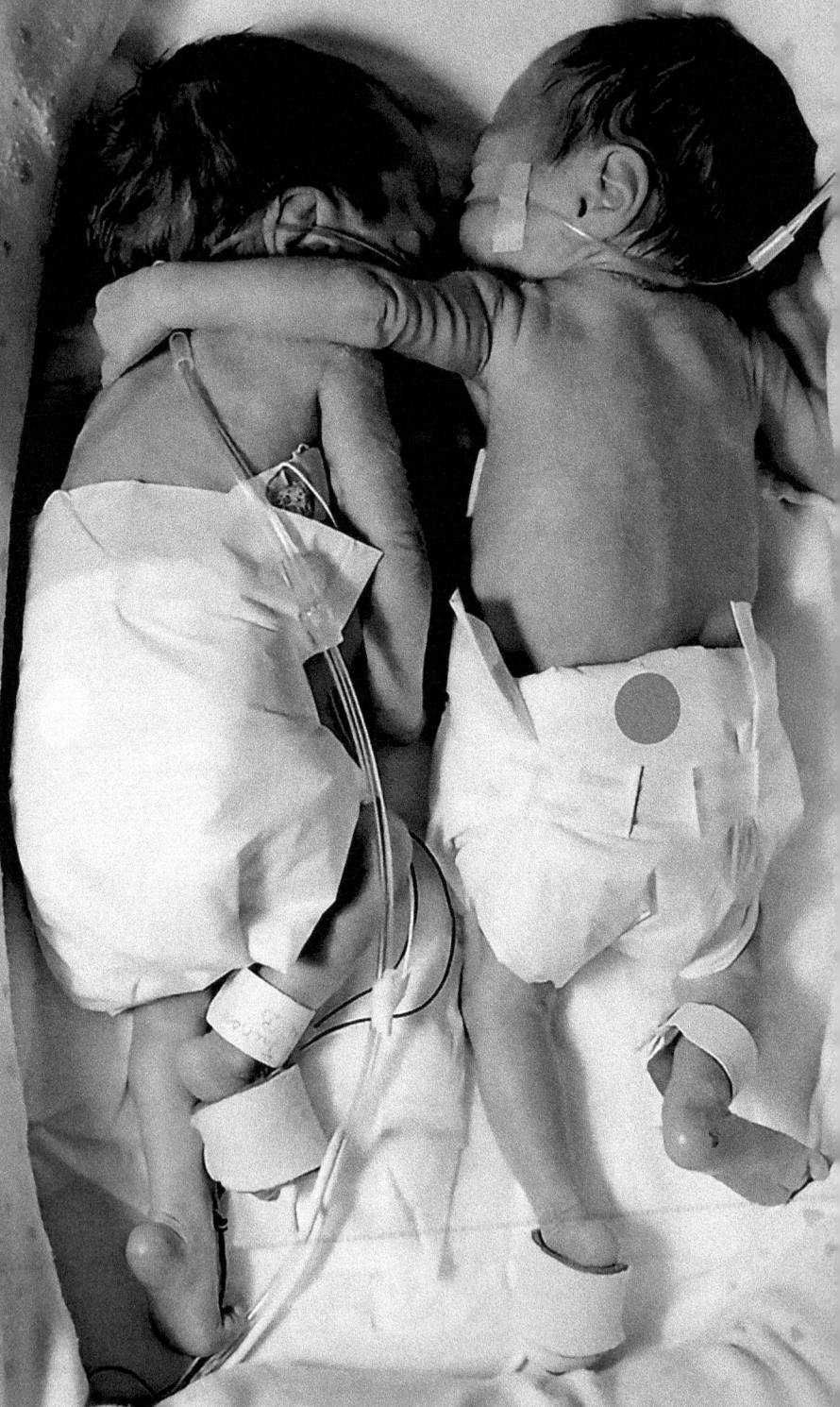

'If two rhythms are nearly the same, and their sources are in close proximity, they will always entrain.'
CHRISTIAN HUYGENS

This is quite an extraordinary phenomenon.

The Russian scientist, Itzhak Bentoff, did further work on this law. His studies showed that when a mother puts her baby on the breast, within a minute or two, the two hearts beat in unison, even though the blood supplies and hearts are separate.

▶ RESCUING HUG

The picture is from an article called 'The Rescuing Hug'.

The article details the first week of life of a set of twins. Each were in their own separate incubator. One was not expected to live. A hospital nurse fought against the hospital rules and placed the babies in one incubator. When they were placed together, the healthier of the two threw an arm over her sister in an endearing embrace. The smaller baby's heart rate stabilised and her temperature rose to normal.

Let us not forget to embrace those whom we love.

To demonstrate the power of this law of entrainment in our workshops, I ask the team to stand in a circle, shoulder to shoulder, facing in towards the centre of the circle. I ask them to hold their arms out and down — with their hands together — so their arms and hands form a pendulum.

Then I ask them to work together as a team, to swing their pendulums from side to side and achieve entrainment.

Everybody independently swings their pendulum from left to right, bumping into the people next to them and it is total chaos.

There is no synchronisation, no entrainment.

Then I ask the leader to call out clear instructions.

So they all lean in with their pendulums — 'left, right, left, right.' Everyone then swings their pendulum to the left and the right in harmony. As they lean in, the feeling in that circle is powerful.

You have probably been on a team working well and entrained. It feels great yet can be challenging to sustain.

Counter-entrainment

Continuing the experiment, I then ask a couple of people to act as counter-entrainers. In their own time, the counter-entrainers swing their pendulums in the opposite direction to the rest of the team.

Within seconds the entrainment of the whole team falls apart.

Then I ask the team — 'Think about your organisation. Who is counter-entraining? Who is working contrary to the spirit of the team?'

Almost everybody can identify somebody who counter-entrained, working against the team spirit. The problem is this. You need only one person on your team counter- entraining to take the team from the smooth harmony of laminar flow to the 40 per cent drop in efficiency that turbulent flow represents. That's how serious this is.

It is treason to your team to allow that person to remain unchallenged. You could have a strong definiteness of purpose and a clear vision. You could be a master of the passion cylinders. You could have outstanding PERT planning rope bridges, but allowing a counter-entrainer to go unchallenged, will negate this.

However, before you remove your counter-entrainers, remember that in chapter fifteen on managing people, we discussed that, when faced with a person not performing, there are five questions to ask:

1. **Do they understand the game — 'let's achieve the vision'?**
2. **Do they know the rules — their personal contribution?**
3. **Are they able to play the game to win — skills and abilities?**
4. **Do they have the chance to play the game — supported with sound systems and culture?**
5. **Do they want to play the game — are they motivated?**

You will need to challenge and counsel any counter-entrainers on the team.

To continue our review of persistence, in the next chapter we'll explore the keys to improving personal persistence.

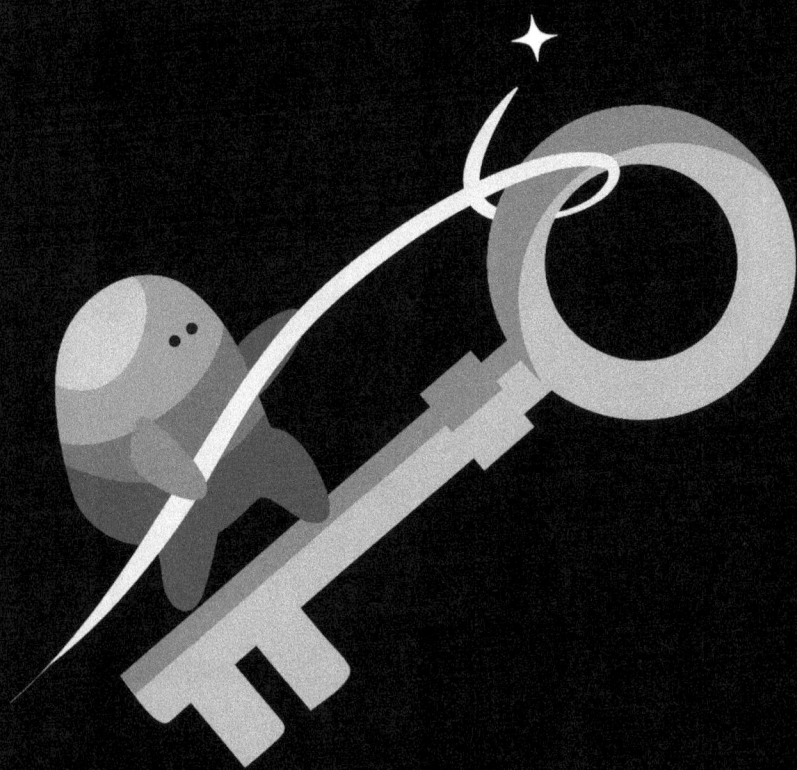

SEVENTEEN

PERSONAL PERSISTENCE KEYS

'It is better to conquer yourself than to win a thousand battles.'
GAUTAMA BUDDHA

The power of persistence is a critical team skill because the resistance aliens will always show up to stand between you and your success.

As we have discussed, team persistence is greatly enhanced by ensuring you have good systems and a supportive culture.

The power of personal persistence is a key leadership quality because, when the going gets tough, people look to you for guidance, inspiration and sometimes raw staying power.

This chapter explores the life journey skills you have to improve the power of your personal persistence and deliver outstanding leadership.

We will do this by reviewing the personal resistance aliens that must be confronted if you wish to develop to the full extent of your management and leadership potential.

▶ PERSONAL RESISTANCE

Do you sometimes find that your personal energy and enthusiasm is failing? Do you find yourself mentally tired and not able to think as clearly as you would like? Is irritability and stress affecting your judgment and your interactions with people around you?

Sure, we all have good days and bad days, but some of us are confronted with such enormous challenges that extra persistence and clarity could distinguish between long-term success or failure.

As 13 of the 16-cylinders of body, mind, emotions and spirit are metaphysical, most of the high leverage keys to reducing personal resistance lie in your metaphysics.

▶ OHM'S LAW RE-VISITED

As we've seen, the laws of physics help us to understand the laws of metaphysics. So let's revisit Ohm's law.

'I' is now the energy and enthusiasm flowing through you. 'V' is the power of your personal vision and your goals. If you want more energy and enthusiasm flowing through you, you need to increase the attraction of your personal vision and the power of your personal goals.

If you have done that to the best of your ability, then the answer that stares at you from Ohm's law is clear, you have to reduce 'R' — your personal resistance.

What does that mean?

▶ LAMINAR AND TURBULENT FLOW RE-VISITED

We have reviewed resistance within a team. When we review personal resistance, it is best to re-visit the example of laminar and turbulent fluid flow.

Remember with a smooth pipe, the water flows through the pipe in a highly efficient lamina flow.

If, however, there's a snag inside the pipe, when the water reaches the snag, it is thrown into turbulent flow. Efficiency is reduced by anywhere between 20%-40%.

So where are the blocks in your personal physical and metaphysical 'pipes'?

Can you afford this potential loss in personal efficiency and life energy?

To answer these questions, we need to review the concept how personal speed is affected by personal resistance.

▶ BMES SPEED

We can return to the 16-cylinder model of body, mind, emotions and spirit to review personal speed.

We are all in motion 'at speed' in body, mind, emotions and spirit. We move around in our environment. Our minds constantly move from thought to thought. Our emotions shift continually. Our spirits are tough and resilient, ever tackling adversity and moving ahead in our life's journey.

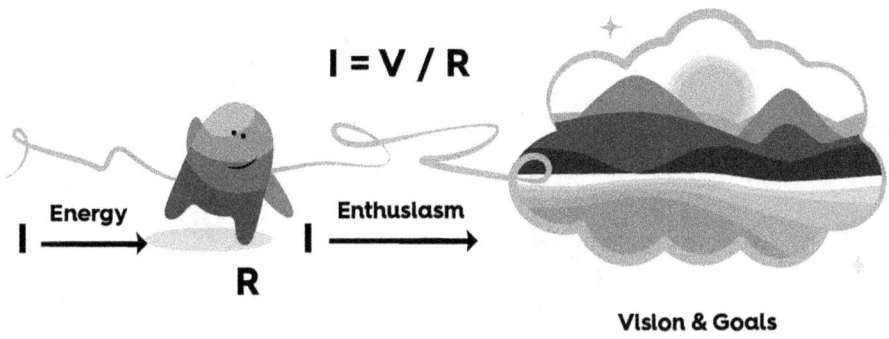

$$I = V / R$$

Energy

R

Enthusiasm

Vision & Goals

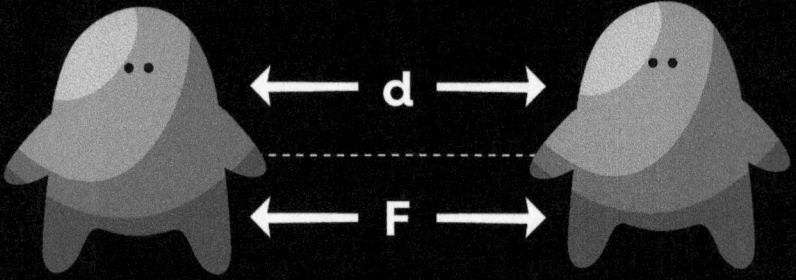

$$F = \frac{G \times M^1 \times M^2}{d^2}$$

V_e = Orbital velocity

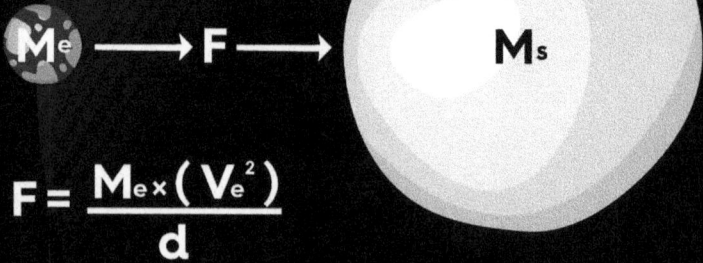

$M_e \longrightarrow F \longrightarrow M_s$

$$F = \frac{M_e \times (V_e^2)}{d}$$

Without that centripetal force of attraction
holding the Earth in orbit,
the Earth would fly off into deep space.

▶ THE RELATIONSHIP LAWS OF METAPHYSICS

In workshops, we often start this section on metaphysical motion and speed by first reviewing interpersonal relationships and then discussing people at work.

Reviewing interpersonal relationships introduces the tools you need to improve your personal persistence.

This approach explores the physics and the metaphysics of relationships both at home and at work.

We have discussed Newton's law of gravity between two physical bodies:

In the diagram, 'Me' is the mass of the Earth. 'Ms' is the mass of the sun — and 'd' is the distance between them.

The gravitational force of attraction 'F', pulling the Earth towards the sun, is a function of the gravitational constant 'G' multiplied by the mass of the Earth 'Me' multiplied by the mass of the sun 'Ms' divided by the square of the distance 'd' between the two bodies.

However the Earth is not stationary, it is in motion as it orbits around the sun.

▶ THE LAW OF CENTRIPETAL FORCE

If we also consider the attraction between two physical bodies in motion, such as our Earth orbiting the sun, or a binary star where the two stars are orbiting each other, there is a second physical law that comes into play. It is the law of centripetal force.

The law of centripetal force states that the force 'F' required to hold an orbiting body, such as the Earth in orbit, is a function of 'Me' — the mass of the Earth multiplied by the square of 'Ve' — its orbital velocity through space — divided by 'd' — the orbital radius — in this case the distance of the Earth from the sun.

For a physical body in motion, such as the Earth orbiting around the sun, the force of gravitational attraction between the Earth and the sun provides the centripetal force that keeps the Earth in orbit.

Without that centripetal force of attraction holding the Earth in orbit, the Earth would fly off into deep space.

▶ RELATIONSHIPS

If we look at two people in a relationship, we move from physics into the realm of unseen metaphysics and the same generalised principles of gravity and centripetal force apply.

When two people originally meet they are in motion, going about their daily lives.

If they are attracted to each other, the law of metaphysical gravity comes into play.

The strength of a metaphysical attraction between two people depends on the distance between them. It's harder to maintain a relationship separated by a large physical distance because the force of inter-attraction reduces by the square of the distance dividing the two people: the tyranny of distance.

You may have experienced the same problem in managing a distant branch of a business.

In Australia, Sydney and Melbourne are only 500 miles apart but Perth is 3000 miles to the west. Getting the Perth team committed to the same vision is hard work. The tyranny of distance is true, proven by Newton's law of gravity — the inter-attraction reduces by the square of the distance. The Perth guys are always doing their own thing. It's not their fault, they just don't feel closely connected to head office.

It will be the same problem for offices on any continent because the law of metaphysical gravity is a generalised principle. It always holds true.

Let's return to our example of two people who are attracted to each other by the law of metaphysical gravity. Because the two people are in motion with speed, the law of centripetal force is also at work. If they form a relationship, they orbit each other.

They stay in motion going about their daily lives but now they are in a relationship.

They share their lives by staying in touch physically, mentally, emotionally and in spirit.

The force of metaphysical gravity, the attraction they feel for each other, provides the centripetal force to keep them orbiting each other in relationship.

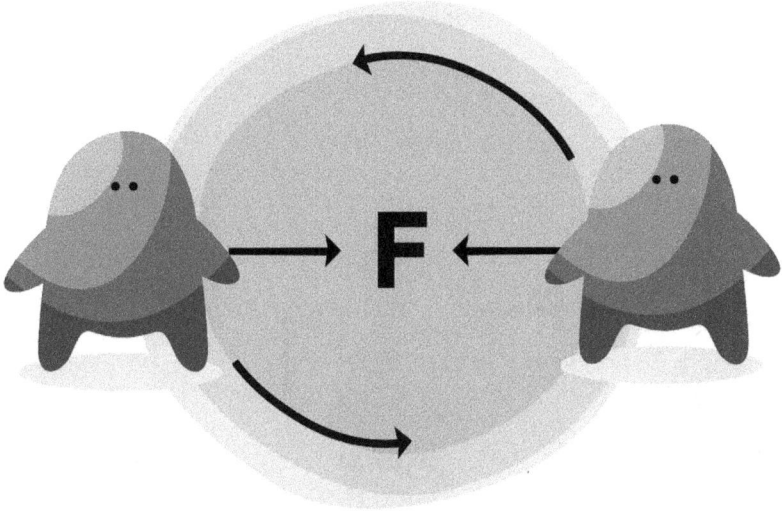

Love

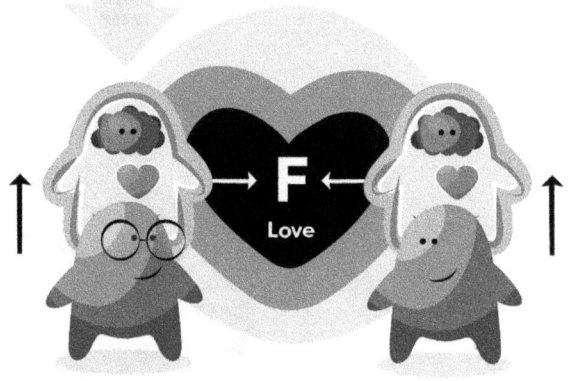

Stable relationships

For a relationship to be stable and last, two people's orbits must be stable. Both need to have similar body, mind, emotions and spirit speeds.

A sports fanatic who loves the outdoor life is unlikely to stay happily in orbit with a couch potato. An emotionally expressive person is unlikely to remain in stable orbit with someone who is withdrawn and dissociated from their feelings.

Two people at similar metaphysical speed will orbit each other in a stable relationship.

As this diagram shows, you and your partner orbit each other because you are both in motion — physically, mentally, emotionally and in spirit. The space in the circle between you is what we call 'love'.

Based on the laws of gravity and centripetal force, to increase the love in your relationship — you need to increase the size of the orbit.

The laws of physics and metaphysics dictate that, to do that, you need to increase your metaphysical mass or speed — or both.

So, in a relationship if you want more love, you both need to increase physical and metaphysical speed. How do you do that? We'll come to that shortly.

Relationship break up

A binary star consists of two stars in motion, orbiting each other. If one of the stars were to suddenly pick up speed, the physical law of centripetal force would predict instability and orbital imbalance.

The same holds true if one partner in a relationship picks up physical or metaphysical speed. If one partner increases speed — and the other does not — the relationship can be thrown into orbital imbalance.

For example, if one partner improves their physical fitness, they will pick up physical speed. If the other partner is happy to remain a couch potato watching television all day, orbital balance may become impossible to maintain.

When severe orbital imbalance occurs, the partners fly apart, the relationship ends and they continue in motion on their own, no longer in orbit around each other. They will then be affected by the laws of metaphysical gravity and motion. They will become attracted to someone of similar metaphysical mass and speed and form a new stable orbit with a new partner who matches their speed.

Teams in orbit

The same gravitational metaphor applies to teams.

Here, the vision can be likened to the sun. The team orbit the vision — held in orbit by the centripetal attraction of the vision.

Various team members can have different metaphysical mass and speed and thus orbit at different radii to the vision — like the planets orbiting the sun.

With teams, the space in the orbits is called trust. A weak vision, slow speeds, small orbits and small metaphysical mass produces low trust. Strong vision, greater centripetal attraction allowing larger metaphysical mass, greater speeds and thus larger orbits — allows more trust.

▶ INCREASING PERSONAL SPEED

Let's look at what could be slowing down your personal speed and what you can do about it. This will increase your personal resilience, energy levels and persistence.

Because you are in motion, your speed is affected by your internal resistance. To increase speed, you need to reduce internal resistance. Resistance of body, mind, emotions and spirit. What does that mean?

Physical body speed

Physical speed is the easiest to start with. If you need to reduce your personal physical resistance — and increase physical speed — you need to ask how fit are you physically?

Do you exercise regularly? If not, commit to improving your physical fitness and schedule in time for exercise.

What about diet, nutrition, hydration and sleep? Are you handling your intake of alcohol in moderation and sensibly? No-one needs to become a fitness fanatic or become extreme about diet, but looking after your body's exercise and nutritional needs is the foundation of good health.

Trust

Act

Our baggage

Improving speed — your physical fitness — is an easy first step to reducing personal resistance.

Spirit speed

People with spirit speed are working with integrity. They don't allow themselves to get caught up in guilt, fear or negativity.

Clarify your life purpose with the twenty five million dollar game.

Take responsibility for your life journey — your growth, your plans, your passions and your relationships. Live with passion and integrity.

Strengthen your own personal ethics. For example, point out a discrepancy in your bill if you are undercharged at a restaurant — play it straight.

Mind and emotions speed

Increasing the clarity and speed of the mind and emotions is about removing the blocks to emotional laminar flow.

To understand these concepts, we need a model:

The core of your being is your spirit, the real you. To access that spirit of awareness, just calm down and observe your body, observe the thoughts streaming through your mind and the ebb and flow of your emotions. That's the spirit you — the watcher, the calm centre of the cyclone of life.

Most of us have created an impressive Act for our daily lives. Our Act is the front we maintain for the world that shows we know what we're doing and we have it together. We all want to appear cool and in control.

However, beneath the surface, we have emotional baggage — the Pain Body. The Pain Body is buried inside our subconscious mind. This is where we store all the pain, all the hurt, all the rejections we have experienced in our lives. It's also where we store all the negative beliefs about ourselves emanating from those painful experiences.

It is as though these negative beliefs are on recorded loops just below our conscious awareness, whispering:

➡ **I'm not good enough**

➡ **Nobody loves me**

→ **I always fail**

→ **I haven't got what it takes**

Occasionally our Pain Body comes up towards the surface of conscious awareness. We have to try to push it back down again — we don't want to feel it. The pain was bad enough the first time!

Our Pain Body clogs our mind and impedes our emotional resilience. It reduces mental and emotional speed. It is our personal resistance. Our emotional baggage hinders our personal persistence.

Our Pain Body can manifest as uneasy, stressful feelings. This is why some people smoke — it's an effective way to suppress unwanted feelings and keep the Pain Body at bay.

When they try and give up smoking, up comes their emotional baggage that the cigarettes effectively suppressed. They feel irritable and yucky, they can't think as clearly and so are strongly tempted to reach for another cigarette to suppress the emotional baggage again. The same goes for people who drink too much or take too many drugs.

Some people put on extra body weight because body weight is useful for suppressing the Pain Body. They hold the negative feelings safely far away in their body mass. Hiding negative emotions in our muscular structure is a wonderful way of not feeling pain.

▶ REDUCING YOUR RESISTANCE — CLEANING UP YOUR EMOTIONAL BAGGAGE

To reduce your personal resistance and turbulence, speed up your mind and improve your emotional resilience, how are you going to deal with the Pain Body?

How are you going to ream out the snags on the inside of your 'pipes' to achieve laminar flow?

How are you going to clean up your inner metaphysics?

Thousands of years ago, the Eastern sages had developed some simple tools and we'll review some of the tools available.

Does it take courage to tackle your Pain Body? Yes.

Is it worth it? I can only speak from the personal experience of myself and my colleagues — and the answer is overwhelmingly yes.

Why would you bother to tackle your own deep subconscious emotional baggage?

Because, as you systematically clean it out, you feel so much better. Your health improves and you have more presence and emotional empathy. Your powers of personal persistence increase significantly.

You become a better leader because the quality of your 'PASS-I-ON' improves.

It is that simple.

To be the most effective leader for your family, your team and your community, you must maximise your own leadership potential. Tackling your own personal Pain Body is the only way forward — but it does require significant personal courage.

Many people prefer to avoid confronting their Pain Body and either choose to be followers or try and lead from their Act. This is not a good strategy as people see through the Act even if it's subconsciously.

To achieve long-term success, you will require persistence, so I urge you to muster the courage to tackle the Pain Body.

Meditation

One of the oldest approaches to cleaning out your emotional baggage is the simple technique of meditation. There are many schools of meditation. All are designed to progressively clear the blocks and focus the mind. A clear mind operates at speed.

There are many meditation apps available online today, some free. Experiment and see which ones work best for you.

You have probably heard of mantras. This is where you repeat a sound, over and over again to calm the mind. When we slow the mind down — from the normally speedy beta wave state to the calmer alpha wave state — it allows the mind to gently release our emotional baggage.

Does this all happen in a day? No.

It takes regular practice. Your Pain Body was created over time, it takes time to clear it out. Meditation is a gentle way of clearing out the emotional baggage in our deeper minds.

Try it and watch how your mental clarity, calmness and resilience under pressure improve as time goes by with the practice of meditation.

Yoga

Yoga is an excellent tool for toning the physical body and stimulating our metaphysical energies.

Our energy centres support and sustain physical health. Yoga exercises 'squeeze out' the emotional baggage held in the muscles. This promotes physical flexibility and clarity of mind.

Bio-energetics

Bio-energetics is an easily learned, simple physical technique for shaking old locked up energies that store emotional baggage out of the body.

There are many other emotional baggage clearing techniques available. The Hindus have a saying – 'When the pupil is ready, the teacher appears.' So, if this area of reducing personal resistance – to increase your personal persistence and speed – interests you, there are hundreds of books and programs out there to guide you. Find one that works for you.

Without clearing your own internal emotional baggage, you may not muster enough persistence to stay the distance. Remember the gold medal standard is getting tougher all the time. All you need is courage and some action to get started.

Fear

➡ False Expectations Appearing Real

The only real enemy is in your mind. You have experienced situations where you have been almost paralysed by fear, however, once you found the courage to face the fear, it wasn't anywhere near as big as you thought it was.

So if you have fear of tackling your emotional baggage, your 'pain body', ask yourself – what is the expectation appearing before me that looks so real? Find the courage to act knowing that the expectation is probably false.

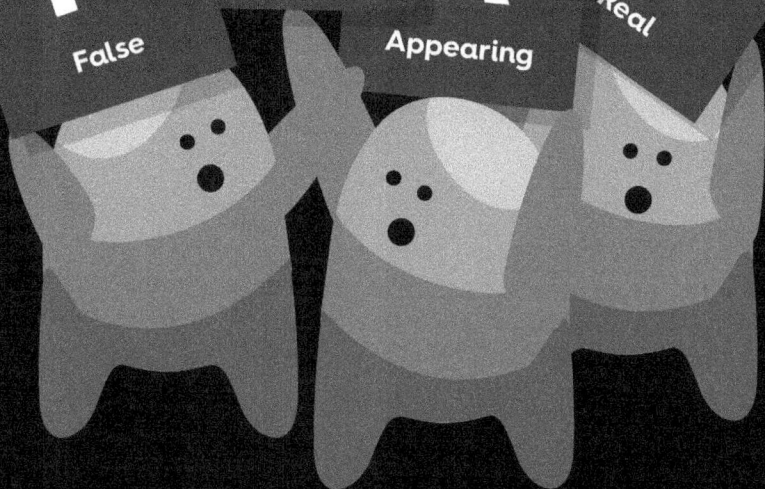

False
Expectations
Appearing
Real

Can you confront and handle your own emotional baggage?

If you do find the courage to do that, then you will have the leadership experience to show the way, to help your team members tackle their own personal resistance — so the entire team can improve personal speed and persistence.

Clearing team emotional baggage

When launching a new product or concept, the marketing message is aimed at innovators. The promotional message is — 'you need this'. Once a market grows, the marketer aims at the opinion leaders with the promotional message — 'it's available'.

Most of your team will probably initially shy away from this very personal concept of clearing out old emotional baggage, reduce personal resistance and increase personal persistence and speed.

Lead by example. Then target the innovators on your team followed by the influencers.

▶ INTENT

Another area that affects personal persistence, as we saw in studying Think and Grow Rich, is the strength of your intent.

The word intent is derived from the Latin 'in tendere' — to stretch towards.

How strong is your intent to succeed, to stretch towards your team vision?

The power of intent comes from the solar plexus where the willpower is focused.

Demonstrating intent is relatively easy when times are good. When times are tough, your will power will be tested. Can you summon the intent to keep working towards your goals and the vision?

Clearing your emotional baggage improves your power of intent. Sometimes the power of your intent may be all that will carry you through against a full scale resistance attack at some point on your life journey.

Optimising your power of intent, and therefore your personal persistence is demonstrating life journey skills in action.

▶ ATTITUDE

Personal persistence is affected by your attitude to big problems.

How do you react to the resistance aliens when they show up?

When the resistance aliens show up, your attitude will define the outcome of the battle. When you're under attack, controlling your emotional state is paramount. Hold the line.

If you focus solely on the problem, you will likely become overwhelmed and sink down into unhelpful, negative emotions.

When the going gets tough, personal persistence means maintaining an attitude of belief in yourself.

Hang in there!

'Everything can be taken from you but one thing: the last of the human freedoms — to choose one's attitude in any given set of circumstances, to choose one's own way.'
VIKTOR FRANKL

▶ RESPONSIBILITY

What is your response-ability, especially in tough times? Who improves your personal persistence? You do.

▶ SUMMARY

Developing the power of personal persistence all comes down to awareness, speed and fitness — fitness of body, mind, emotions and spirit. It doesn't matter what emotional baggage you're carrying from your past, you can heal and cleanse the Pain Body.

As you clear out your old emotional baggage, laminar energy flow replaces turbulent energy flow and your energy and persistence increase significantly.

As your energy goes up, that energy gets passed on as charisma, motivation and inspiration to your team.

How serious are you in realising your full life and leadership potential?

EIGHTEEN

YOUR FUTURE

'I feel that luck is preparation meeting opportunity.'
OPRAH WINFREY

▶ LUCK AND PREPAREDNESS

Who knows what opportunities your life journey will present to you? So always work on your preparedness.

Achieve mastery in life and business

You now understand the need for a definiteness of purpose. You have developed a graphical vision. You've learned about the keys to inspiring passion, motivation and enthusiasm.

You understand the need for clear plans of action and then working back from the future using the graphical PERT planning tool and asking — what happened just before that?

We have explored persistence. There is team persistence — underpinned by good systems and a supportive culture. There is also personal persistence which can be improved by reducing personal resistance.

These tools provide you with life journey mastery skills.

▶ YOUR COMMITMENTS TO CHANGE

Now is the time to establish and then regularly check your Commitments Register.

You are now armed with a set of practical tools to help you, and the people around you, tap hidden advantages and go confidently forward and succeed.

What are your commitments to change? Check them now.

▶ THE POWER OF COMMITMENT

This often-published quote from WN Murray of the 1951 Scottish Himalayan Expedition may reinforce to you the power of commitment:

Commitment

'Until one is committed, there is hesitancy, the chance to draw back, always ineffectiveness. Concerning all acts of initiative (and creation) there is one elementary truth, the ignorance of which kills countless ideas and splendid plans: that the moment one commits oneself, then Providence moves too. All sorts of things occur to help one that would otherwise never have occurred.

A whole stream of events issues from the decision, raising in one's favour all manner of unforeseen incidents and meetings and material assistance, which no man could have dreamt would have come his way. I have learned a deep respect for one of Goethe's couplets — Whatever you can do, or dream you can, begin it. Boldness has genius, power and magic in it.'

WN MURRAY, 1951 SCOTTISH HIMALAYAN EXPEDITION

Record your commitment to change in your Commitments Register for clarity and future reference.

▶ THANK YOU

Finally, let me say how much I admire your persistence in working through this book. You are on a journey through life. You have something significant yet to do and you have something special inside you, something unique, a gift with which you can make a difference.

If this book has helped you towards life mastery, it has served its purpose. As you now continue on your journey, I offer you my personal best wishes. GO FOR IT!!

www.ingramcontent.com/pod-product-compliance
Lightning Source LLC
Chambersburg PA
CBHW051942090426
42741CB00008B/1243